An Unholy Conspiracy

The Scandal of
the Separation of Church and Industry
since the Reformation

MALCOLM GRUNDY

The Canterbury Press
Norwich

British Library Cataloguing in Publication Data

A catalogue record for this book is available
from the British Library

ISBN 1-85311-029-9

*Typeset by Cambridge Composing (UK) Ltd
Printed and bound in Great Britain by
St Edmundsbury Press Limited
Bury St Edmunds, Suffolk*

To Wendy and Stephen

By the same author:

LIGHT IN THE CITY

Foreword

I am most grateful for the opportunity to commend this book and hope it will help to bring a better understanding of the relationship between industry and the church, between the work ethic and Christian principle.

Soundly based in theological experience, the author provides a splendid tie-in of the economic and the spiritual with his *reflective practice* sequence and in describing the terms 'Spiritual Liberation' and 'Ethical Liberation'. This fresh and provocative presentation of the theme deserves a wide readership.

The Rt Revd Peter Walker

The Social Reformer

Cartoon from *The Evening Standard*, April 1943.

Contents

ACKNOWLEDGEMENTS

Thanks are due to the following for permission to quote from copyright sources: the editors of *Crucible* for permission to re-use extracts from my articles on Industry Year and on Conflict; Pelican books and Random Century Group for permission to use material from Terry Coleman's *The Railway Navvies* and to Pelican books for permission to use material from *The Church in an Age of Revolution* by Alec Vidler. I am grateful to Coracle books for permission to quote a passage from Dick Sullivan's *Navvyman*.

I have used with permission an extract on Worker Priests in *The Church and Industrial Society* by Gregor Siefer, published by Darton, Longman and Todd, and an extract about Industrial Mission from *Church and People in an Industrial City* by E. R. Wickham published by Lutterworth.

The Sheffield Industrial Mission has been kind enough to allow me to use extensive material from *Industrial Mission in Sheffield Revisited* by Philip Bloy. I have been allowed to use equally long extracts from *Requiem for American Industrial Missions* which is an Audenshaw Paper by the Revd Scott Paradise. Finally, I am grateful to the Industrial Christian Fellowship for permission to revise the substance of an article on the debate about intermediate technology and growth which was published in *The I.C.F. Quarterly*.

M. G.

Introduction

The churches and the industries of Britain occupy separate worlds. This book explores a theory, an idea, which I have developed over the past twenty years as I have occupied a small place in both these worlds. It is that to a large extent church and industry are happy that their worlds are separate. More than that, my exploration and my experiences of these worlds leads me to conclude not only that church and industry are content with their separation but also that they have colluded in a series of conspiracies to maintain the situation. Hence the title of this book and the theory which I want to explore which points to a conspiracy of separation. It is not a deliberate and planned conspiracy but a conspiracy of convenience.

Christian churches have an awkwardness with the use of money and even more so about the making of profits by industrial or commercial activity. Through the centuries has grown the idea that this world of hard decisions, of competition and compromises, is a dirty world and one in which Christians find it hard to work with an easy conscience. Equally the world of industry and commerce has developed its own business practices and its own codes of behaviour on an international scale. It does not welcome interference from outside agencies, least of all churches which dare to challenge their methods of operation and the effects of their actions on a wider society. Each is content to keep the other well at arm's length.

Such a separation cannot produce an integrated and participative society. Christians should not be happy that one whole section of God's creation is regarded as almost beyond the redemptive process. Indeed such a conception is amazing if we hold to the idea that human beings are made in God's image and that we are in some way stewards and workers in the continuing activity of creation.

In the past two centuries there is a brave history of individuals and organisations who have tried to bridge the gap between the two communities. The Navvy Mission, the Christian Social Union, the Industrial Christian Fellowship and hundreds in the industrial mission movement have made their inroads. Some continue today. But theirs is not a story of lasting achievements or of a modified situation. One reason for this lack of influence is the rapidly changing nature of society which makes attempts to tackle social questions seem outdated very quickly. More significant a reason has been the bias in the churches against anything other than the parochial, pastoral, idea of ministry. This feeds the idea in industry that Christianity is only about individual problems, about 'welfare', and not about the structures and working practices which may well contribute to those problems. I have been led again and again in looking at these caricatures of Christianity, and living in them, to consider this theory that we are each maintaining what I regard to be an 'unholy conspiracy'.

Very much more important is the consequence of this conspiracy for the vast majority of adult Christians who have to work for a living. If they are engaged in a productive, wealth-creating industry, if they deal in money or if they have senior jobs in 'big business' or the trades unions, very often they are made to feel guilty by their churches, through sermons and in much literature, for doing their jobs at all. It may be true that some jobs are an offence to the Christian conscience. In that case believers do need to be challenged about what they are doing. For most working people this is not the case. Christians do not need to be made guilty about what they do and to feel that they are only of real value for what they contribute to the church, in their family, and in their social lives. Something has gone terribly wrong if Christians cannot offer up to God what they do in one of the main areas of their lives. This book sets out to expose what are in fact a series of conspiracies and to suggest spiritual and practical ways in which an integration of faith and work can be achieved.

There will be some who have been working in this area for a long time who will say that there is nothing new in this book. Many colleagues who have worked at these questions will recognise previous discussions and writings. But I am convinced that when our ideas are put together *in this particular way* they will make the reasoning sharper and will explain how these conspiracies have frustrated many of our past efforts or given them only short-lived success.

I owe debts of gratitude to a vast array of people who have supported me in my thinking on these matters while I have been an industrial missioner, an adult educator and a parish priest. There are more than I can list but many will recognise their influence in what I say. While the influence may be theirs the responsibility for what is written in this way is entirely my own. I am grateful particularly to the Sheffield Industrial Mission for the formative years I spent as a chaplain there. The Industrial Christian Fellowship has kept a hold on me and supported me through the very different years of the 1980s. The consultations I have attended at St George's House, Windsor, have enabled me to meet people and share ideas which otherwise I would only have read about. My thanks go to these groups in particular.

The manuscript was read by Mr Don Hood, the Rt Revd Peter Walker and Canon Peter Ball, and I am grateful for their helpful comments. Gordon Knights and Kenneth Baker of The Canterbury Press Norwich have had confidence in the subject matter of this book from the outset. My gratitude to them is enormous for their trust in allowing me to put these ideas into a more public arena.

It is my hope that after reading this book many will see exposed the roots of one of the major problems of our society. Perhaps many more will come to see the centrality of work as we have it and of wealth creation as a vital element in our economy. With a renewed confidence in these ideas I am sure that poor and rich will gain much more help. Most of all, I hope that in and through our work many more of us will be able to see God's creative hand in everything that we do.

Malcolm Grundy

Chapter One

Who wants to work?

Almost everyone has to work for a living. Most of those too rich to need a job still want to do something useful with their lives. Most of those who are unfortunate enough to be unemployed wish they had a job. We want to work and to get a whole range of satisfactions from it. So why is it that more of us do not get up each morning and go off with enthusiasm to a job we enjoy? Why is our country not full of people dedicated to their work? Why are not more of our companies bursting with new ideas and producing high quality, reliable, products at competitive prices, the envy of the rest of the world — or at least of Japan, Germany, the United States?

Even more absurdly, why is it not obvious to everyone that God is at the centre of all creation? Surely to be creative at work is to live in God's image? Anyone who is sensitive and steeped in the centuries old Christian culture of the west ought to know and understand this. Offering motor cars and planes, computers and fax machines to God as the fruits of human labour should be as natural as loving one's children. But it is not.

The reasons for the 'credibility gap' between what Christians might hope for and what is true may be obvious if taken at the level of experience in the unfair lottery we call life. For many people work is boring, unpleasant, unfulfilling and badly paid. It is the lucky few who have interesting jobs and who can say with varying degrees of modesty 'I am lucky to be paid so well for doing what is really my hobby'.

There is a great gulf between idealised hopes for Christian

attitudes to work and the *experience* of very many people in the work they have to do. Whatever William Blake meant by Dark Satanic Mills — he might have meant the spires of Oxford — it is the mills, factories, production lines and coal mines of Victorian England that have become embedded in many people's minds as the epitome of all that is bad about industry and commerce.

Today, very few people work for themselves, although the number starting small businesses is growing. More and more of us work in companies which are part of other companies, which were taken over by other companies who in turn are part of multi-national companies. One consequence of these spider's webs is that we can use the term 'industry' to talk about much wider patterns of employment. We even talk of the health industry, the education industry as well as the food industry and the agricultural industry and the banking industry! So, in this discussion about attitudes to work and 'Church and industry', this wider meaning will be intended. The terms 'industry' or 'industry and commerce' will be used to describe attitudes to whatever might be considered as our work, the principal gainful occupation of most of us from school or college to retirement. However, emphasis will be placed on attitudes to those employed in the 'wealth-creating' industries and the history of the particular response the churches have tried to make to them through the centuries.

The origins of a conspiracy theory

I have worked as a farm-hand in a flower nursery, as a labourer in a brewery, as a draughtsman in an architect's office as well as an employee in the 'industry' of organised religion in the Church of England. For all of that time it feels as if I have been sitting, or standing, alongside a wide range of people who have wanted to talk about their work. They have done so freely and naturally, many of them relieved that at last there was someone really interested in what they are doing. As a visitor to large factories and to many offices I have always been surprised at how much time can be found to talk without work being affected as a machine continues to run or a chemical process takes its course. As a comparatively young industrial chaplain I was surprised that senior managers would tell their secretaries to cross out time in the diary so that we could talk in an uninterrupted way. Never did we gossip about other people, often we discussed the pressures facing a company and its employees. On many occasions we discussed the effect of this particular kind of work on the people involved.

For a while I was happy to leave things at that and be grateful that I was available to be used as a sounding board or just as blotting paper to soak up the descriptions of all that was being shared. But after a while I began to think that this was not enough. A deep recession hit our proud city of Sheffield and whatever people tried to do they were helpless victims of forces much stronger than themselves which were altering the shape of their industry. Like many other traditional industries in Britain, steel and coal were no longer as competitive as they once were. The fault clearly was not only with those who were running those industries at that time. It went back for generations. I began to see how much our national attitudes to industry were caught up with the nature of our country, its social divisions and its educational structure. I was hit by a phrase used by Sir Geoffrey Chandler, Director of Industry Year, 1986, that we are 'an industrial country with an anti-industrial culture'.

I had not yet at this stage arrived at the 'conspiracy theory' but I was becoming aware that attitudes to work run very deep. The very great national alarm at the prospect of there being three million people unemployed in our country was universal. People spoke of unemployment as a 'cancer'. There was something about work, and no work, which affected people's spirit in a way which they found hard to express because these feelings, these emotions, were coming new to the surface. While showing an interest in industry not before realised I had the profound spiritual connection between work and human development or formation.

A public conspiracy debate

In the mid 1980s I became drawn into a more public debate about attitudes to industry when the Royal Society of Arts Manufacturers and Commerce mounted a national campaign to try and change attitudes to work. They declared 1986 'Industry Year' with two slogans, 'Thanks to Industry' and 'Industry Matters'. Even within the ranks of Christian supporters of close links between church and industry there were strong voices for and against. Advocates and opponents from the churches met for combat at St George's House in Windsor Castle early in 1985. Giving his 'Yes' and 'No' to Industry Year, Canon Martin Wright, Chairman of the Industrial Mission Association said, 'No — to an Industry Year if it is nothing more than a bland promotional exercise to baptise the unacceptable faces of industry — that is not the church's business.

'No — to a press handout which implies that the only things which need to be changed are other people's hostile *attitudes* to industry, rather than their *experience* of industry itself on which those attitudes are based. People's *attitudes* are likely to change when their *experience* changes.

'No — to a campaign which asks people to affirm something which in their own experience is frequently akin to vandalism. For many people "industry" means strikes, disruption of services, violence on the picket lines; it still means factory chimneys and dirt, unemployment and inequality, mass production and shift work, profitability at all costs, a cuckoo which offers goodies to a community, makes them dependent on it, takes what it wants, and then disappears with the proceeds. For many people "industry" means that combination of interests which holds the power to destroy the only way of life they know.

'So, no — to a slogan "Thanks to Industry" which seems oblivious to this aspect of our corporate experience and lacks even the grace to cover itself with a question mark. "Thanks to Industry?", question mark, would at least give recognition to the *ambiguity* of our attitudes to industry. As it is, most of the people I have spoken to greet it with a hollow laugh.'

Fierce in defence of the idea of an Industry Year was 'Ted' Wickham, former Bishop of Middleton, who in 1944 had founded the Sheffield Industrial Mission.

He argued, '. . . Christian faith, biblical faith, affirms the "Providential" character of the creation, and the call of mankind, through science, technology and industry, to utilise the potentials of creation "for the glory of God and the relief of man's estate," as Francis Bacon superbly put it many years ago . . . The moral imperative for the responsible making of wealth and its right use, or to put it another way, the use of the immense technological power now in our hands in the service of a good social order stems from the Biblical understanding of God and His will for mankind — as our power increases, so the demands of love, understanding and sensitivity take on a critical urgency.'

These differing positions highlight some of the ways we can talk about work. They range from the careers optimism we use for school leavers or graduates to the bitterness of experience rising from forty years of unfulfilled toil, strikes, redundancies and take-overs.

Why are so many people disillusioned with work? Is it just their bad experiences or are they aided and abetted, conditioned, in their responses by an inherited 'anti-industrial culture' which runs like a faulty seam through the bedrock of British, or more likely English, society?

Industry Year prodded the churches, or at least some people within the churches, to join in a national debate about attitudes to work and to Britain as a declining industrial action. Few people saw this as a spiritual dilemma. When discussions in the local church took place they were characterised very often by discussions of the Wright-Wickham kind. People debated the question whether or not what they knew of work made it impossible for Christians to speak optimistically about it or to imagine any kind of fulfilling employment in the future. In later chapters I shall explore some of the effects of pressure groups within the churches who have contributed to an anti-industrial bias.

Because of the social background of many who go to church discussion about work had a 'middle-class', professional, feel to it. Inevitably there was little experience to share of manual labour or of the repetitiveness of many mechanical processes, though women could contribute something of the frustrations of being kept at the lower levels of responsibility in employment. Interestingly, many who began their working lives as teachers or in the health-care industry or as 'staff' now began to speak about their disillusionment with the career they had chosen. The personal, spiritual, sense of fulfilment they had hoped for had not been forthcoming because, in many cases, the job had changed beyond all recognition.

Where had the churches been while all these changes were going on? There was little evidence of a healthy debate about the changing nature of technology and of employment and even less about the way in which situations of stress and of radical changes in job structure could be offered up to God. There was more of the sense of 'we told you so' and an encouragement to close ranks and find personal fulfilment within the closer fellowship of the churches.

Those of us who had stood alongside people under pressure as changes took place and who had been very active in trying to develop new employment schemes for teenagers and for adults began to wonder what was happening within our churches. Instead of a brave exploration of the possibilities for reconstruction which new technologies could bring, churches were content to foster a private faith and to enjoy an amazing conscience-free criticism of the harmful effects of industry and commerce. It was then that I began to realise how much more comfortable it was to keep at arm's length from these difficult changes than it was to become involved in a positive and constructive way. Equally disturbing was the experience that those involved in spearheading change saw little advantage in the churches taking any interest in their work at all. There was indeed an unorganised, yet convenient, collusion on both sides that the two worlds of church and industry were better kept apart.

The argument for a conspiracy

I first came to consider the case for a series of conspiracies in a systematic way when I read a book by Martin Weiner called *English culture and the decline of the industrial spirit 1850–1980*.[1] He says that church leaders have been as guilty as others in not wanting to accept the reality of the working lives of most people in this country. His book argues that the Industrial Revolution did not establish a new industrial elite in Britain. Industrialisation created a new class of aristocratic capitalists when the landed gentry made capital no longer from their estates but from their factories and mines. The values and culture of the old landowning class who were not overthrown by industrialisation allowed a peaceful accommodation to take place which actually entrenched romantic sentiments about arts, culture and idyllic rural village life. It was the embodiment of these values which ennobled the true Englishman.

Such an accommodation was encouraged by another nineteenth-century social trend, the gentrification of the Victorian middle classes. Between 1841 and 1881 the population of Britain rose by 60% while membership of the seventeen main professions — among them lawyers, doctors, public officials, journalists, men of letters, professors and clergy[2] — rose by

150%. Such people, educated almost entirely by the new Public Schools system, established a professional upper-middle class with similar cultural values to set alongside the aristocratic industrial capitalists. They made working in 'trade' or 'industry' dirty words.

Through the development of the novels of Dickens, the preference for Gothic architecture, the influence of William Morris and John Ruskin, the 'Merrie England' ideals of many socialists, and the lives of leading politicians, Baldwin the steelowner and country gentleman, being a classic example, Martin Weiner traces this refusal to accept the values and culture of industrial invention and production. He sees the Great Exhibition of 1851 as the high water mark and the beginning of the end of Britain's inventive spirit. The deaths of Brunel, Stevenson and Locke within a few months of each other in 1859–60 are for him the end of an era.

Leading churchmen in the first half of this century are seen as co-conspirators by Weiner. He looks at the writings of a conservative churchman like Dean Inge who clearly thought that England had been diverted from its true nature by the industrial revolution. The Conference on Christian Politics, Economics and Citizenship (COPEC)in 1924 is also examined. Weiner sees its membership as drawn chiefly from the professions and the voluntary social services and concludes, 'Its reports over the following few years, laid out a wide-ranging critique of capitalism, set in a historical frame by R. H. Tawney, a leading member. Nostalgia for the Middle Ages and for the crafts and recreations of an idealised, earlier age permeated COPEC.'[3]

It is possible to see in this interpretation of our social history the seeds of the support which many Christians give today to 'small is beautiful', to intermediate technology and alternative communities. They lead to the outright condemnation by some Christians of large industries and of trans-national corporations. The less than enthusiastic response towards industry and commerce from many in the churches may well be the result of this anti-industry cultural inheritance.

If this argument is in any way true then there is an urgent need for the churches to look again at these inherited attitudes. It may seem a little dramatic to describe this willing separation of church and industry as an 'unholy conspiracy' but such a polarisation does help to sharpen the argument. It may also help to explain the failure of many attempts to integrate work and the Christian faith in the past. The lack of a spiritual dimension may well explain why work is seen as a major cause of secularisation. I shall explore this accusation in chapter seven. Most importantly the exposure, or understanding, of a conspiracy will be the first step towards a real coming together of the spiritual and the practical aspects of our lives and be a real support to believers and unbelievers alike as they search for an integrity within the work that they do.

We have a problem

One thing is certain. In Britain we do have a problem about attitudes to work. Unless the main opinion-formers in our society begin to address it, what hope is there that our children will get up and go to work with any more enthusiasm than we do ourselves?

In 1990 when advice was being given to university entrants on receipt of their good or bad 'A' level results they were told that places were tight for medicine and the law, courses in French and German were quite full, but anyone with two grade E's at 'A' level would be able to find a place on a course in electrical engineering. Little has changed in fifty, or even, a hundred years!

Chapter Two

An unholy conspiracy?

How did we get into this mess? How is it that the social aims and religious life of a nation can become so out of tune with the economic events which actually shape its life? Is anyone to blame? Perhaps we should try to blame the Bishops and the politicians. We are all familiar with the political posturing of both! In the short-term political life of governments it can be made to look as if the policies of one party cause so much damage that it takes almost the whole of the first term of an incoming government to put them right. Then, in a second term new strides begin to be made but some totally unforeseen problem comes over the horizon and progress is frustrated yet again, and so the cycle continues. In the life of a Diocese or a parish things are usually slightly more veiled, but hardly any different.

Explanations, excuses and blame for the state of our nation abound. We are the victims of changes of policy of other, stronger, nations. The Dollar and the Yen influence the Pound. The E.E.C. now locks Britain into a monetary system and cramps our style. In the wide world of trade we do know, of course, that it is cheaper and easier to produce many goods closer to the source of raw materials and consequently we have lost much of our manufacturing base and many of our markets.

Yet we also know that our competitor countries facing these, or greater, disasters have risen from their ashes and have made economic recoveries and have developed new products in a way that Britain has found impossible. What is the weakness in our economic thinking which creates a self-destructive urge, or at least makes us unable to redevelop what we have or to make a commercial success of our new ideas?

Recently some Japanese researchers looked at the success of the hundred most successful companies across the world. They found that the ideas which sustain over half of them came from Britain but were taken over by companies in competitor countries. Why were we not able to develop more of these ourselves? Was the competition from overseas too great? Were research and development departments better overseas? We do not, and have never, lacked inventiveness. What we appear to lack is the ability to believe in our ideas enough to invest in them and work day and night to promote them against all opposition. Do we really have what our competitors call 'the British Disease'? If we do, what are its origins, and how can we begin to put things right?

Who can we blame?

I suggested that we should blame the Bishops as well as the politicians because I think that the place both of our Christian leaders — Bishops, theologians and clergy — and also of our political thinkers and leaders is linked and, that just perhaps, they have conspired together to allow some of our problems to develop and to persist.

It may at first seem dull to many to suggest that we go right back to the roots of our modern social and religious history for explanations. I am sure that we need to do this so that we can explore properly the origins of our difficulties over attitudes to industry and commerce, to making and selling things. In this way I hope that we shall see more clearly, perhaps for the first time, where some of our present difficulties lie. One almost forgotten theologian and social commentator from the beginning of this century, J. N. Figgis, says that the seeds of our twentieth-century economic problems were sown before the Reformation and did not begin to bear their fruit until after the Civil War. I am sure he was right.

The lessons of history

A better known economic historian, R. H. Tawney, has developed the argument in a full and most persuasive way in *Religion and the rise of capitalism*[1] a book which was first published in 1926 and has stood the test of time to become a classic and a foundation book for anyone interested in this question.

He argues that the Church of the Middle Ages was a tremendous unifying organisation. It spanned a Europe which had many features of a single society with structures and laws originating in the Roman Empire, which were welded together within the rigid structure of feudalism. A distinctive feature of Christian medieval thought, explains Tawney, is that contrasts which were later thought to be irreconcilable, appear then as differences within a larger unity. The sinful nature of this world was assumed by the church but God offered the possibility of forgiveness both to individuals and institutions alike by the ministry of grace offered through the church. Social institutions as well as individuals felt the incarnated presence of God in their activities. From the documents, art and architecture of the time this seems to be by no means a romantic opinion.

The idea of an over-arching moral and social unity goes some way to explain the theories of leading churchmen and reformers like Luther and Calvin in mainland Europe, and in England of Anglicans like Latimer and Laud, Non-Conformists like Bunyan and Quakers like Bellers. Teachings about how people should live and work in a new kind of society were produced by men whose ideas had recognisable medieval parents. Their thinking and their responses to the changes which were going on around them stem from this concept of an integrated Europe and a Christendom which saw faith, church and a revised view of the sacraments as means of redeeming individuals and institutions from a fallen society. They saw rulers and merchants, church and state as co-equals with separate functions set within the divine plan of salvation.

Their ideas were not to find a happy home. The fifteenth, sixteenth and seventeenth centuries in which they lived saw the coherence of European society breaking down. There grew up a new kind of trading with wider markets. Banking grew in prominence. There was a newly-emerging middle-class of merchants in the towns. Renaissance princes wanted their nation states. Central control, of morality as well as economics, from Rome or anywhere else was resented, and in northern Europe overthrown.

Fuelled by this great burst of economic, political and religious activity feudal society collapsed under the pressure as rapidly as Victorian society crumbled after the First World War. The changes in society which were taking place were first charted by the German sociologist Max Weber with a thesis set out in another fundamental work, *The protestant ethic and the spirit of capitalism.*[2] It was much used by Tawney and others in the United Kingdom.

The protestant business ethic

Weber observed that certain fundamental changes were taking place in the underlying ethical behaviour of the new traders, bankers and businessmen. He saw that the business leaders, higher grades of skilled labour and higher trained personnel in any country of mixed Christian allegiances were predominantly protestant. He concluded that the underlying attitude of mind of protestants was different. He saw that their attitudes of mind were more dynamic than those in any previous European trading system. A search for the origin of these attitudes led Weber to the Reformation and to the concept of 'calling'. He says, 'The idea of calling is the product of the Reformation and one thing was unquestionably new; the valuation of the fulfilment of duty in worldly affairs as the highest form of moral activity.' To Luther, 'to labour in a calling appears as the outward expression of brotherly love' in contrast with monasticism's selfish renunciation of temporal obligations. Weber contrasted this attitude with the hand-to-mouth existence of the peasant; the privileged traditionalism of the guild craftsman and adventurer's capitalism, re-orientated to the exploitation of political opportunities and irrational speculation. He concluded that the restraints which were made upon the consumption of wealth by insistence on a simple life-style made possible the productive investment of capital. Going deeper into the theological basis of 'calling', Weber said that the protestant identifies true faith by objective results, by conduct which serves to increase the glory of God. Conviction of a person's own salvation cannot, as in Catholicism, consist in a gradual accumulation of good works to one's credit, but rather in a systematic self-control. God demanded not single good works but a life of good works combined into a unified system. There was no place for the very human medieval cycle of sin, repentance, atonement and release, followed by renewed sin.

Calling and Calvinism

Tawney looked more closely into the concept of 'calling' in Calvinism, at its establishment and growth within what became the middle class communities of Europe and North America. He goes on from Calvinism to talk of a Puritan spirit of morality. The labour of a Puritan moralist, he says, is not merely an economic means to be laid aside when physical needs have been satisfied. It is a spiritual end and must be continued as an ethical duty long after it has ceased to be a material necessity.

By the early nineteenth century the dangers of such thinking were becoming apparent. The demand for success in business and for profit was becoming rapidly divorced from its religious and spiritual origins. Puritanism was replaced by Utilitarianism, a danger anticipated by John Wesley himself. In a sermon on riches he says, 'Religion must necessarily produce both industry and frugality, and these cannot but produce riches. But as riches increase, so will pride, anger and love of the world. How then is it possible that Methodism, that is a religion of the heart, though it flourishes now as a green bay tree, should continue in this state? For the Methodists in every place grow diligent and frugal; consequently they increase in goods. Hence they proportionately increase in pride, anger, in the desire of the flesh, the desire of the eyes and the pride of life. So, although the form of religion remains, the spirit is rapidly vanishing away.'

Helpless victims or co-conspirators?

Were the churches, traditional and reformed, or completely new, helpless victims of the changes which were going on around them or were they co-conspirators in a willing pact to keep spheres of moral activity separate in just the same way that home and work were becoming separated?

The churches spawned by the Reformation had a much less developed system for thinking about corporate activity but were based much more on a personal, private, internalised faith which was ill-fitted for the country house religion of the squire — high and dry — or for the mechanical systems of the factory. Calvin's 'experiment' of regulating both secular and religious life in Geneva burst under the pressure of trying to integrate business, civic and personal life in one harmonised but autocratic community.

It still seems strange to me to go to the Cathedral in Geneva and see the seats of the city councillors placed in the semi-circular apse of the sanctuary where once the altar had stood. Why is there to my twentieth-century mind an awkwardness in seeing things set out in this way? It is certainly not a case of the moneychangers in the temple, though the similarity does need to be explored. It is more the conditioning of a modern mind to the unholy conspiracy which we are examining which runs deep in our culture from that time. The uneasiness which has more validity is in the forcing together of separated functions. This falseness pretending to be harmony prevents the real opportunity to examine a legitimate code of behaviour for each which can then be used to recognise responsible activities which can then be allowed to act co-operatively under God.

Usury and the moneylenders

Handling and dealing in money has caused anxiety in Christians from the earliest days and there is a strong tradition of poverty and the renunciation of worldly goods in much of our spirituality. With the development of trading on a much larger scale the handling of money, and the lending of it, had to be faced by Christian businessmen. There is evidence that double-entry book-keeping was in use before the Reformation and that there was some lending of money at interest. The unpopularity of the medieval Jews was in part that they had been the moneylenders. Not allowed to charge interest to fellow Jews by Psalm 15 and by the Mosaic Law, Exodus 22.25 and Deuteronomy 23.19–20, the Gentiles posed them no such problems.

In the early church usury gradually came to be regarded as unlawful and was condemned by the Third Lateran Council in 1179. The reasoning was based on Aristotle's argument about the barren use of money. The medieval attitude to usury, as well as having a biblical basis, was related to the doctrine of the just price. The essence of the argument was that in any transaction justice demanded an equivalent return by the buyer to the seller. Where money was lent it was held that the mere passage of time did not reduce the value of money and hence gave rise to no claim for more than repayment of the principal. In the same medieval frame Martin Luther condemned all taking of interest. He held that money was unproductive and should not multiply itself without work.

It was Calvin who broke this mould and who gave a Christian justification for the rampant commercial activity which traders in Geneva and in many places elsewhere had begun. Calvin said that interest should be allowed if it were for the good of the community as a whole. It may seem like splitting hairs, but he distinguished between a productive loan and usury. He said that to lend money to increase capital, to make production possible, was not a sin. In that use money was just as productive as any other merchandise. In Calvin's explanation of his teaching we can see that he was by no means justifying the new individualism but was still in the mould of those who had gone before him. He did not link individualism with free-enterprise. He linked economic activity to the needs of the community as a whole, connecting the duty a person owes to God with a duty to the whole community — and with all human endeavour. The teaching legitimised current practice without really speaking to the morality of those engaging in this commercial activity. They took what they wanted and were allowed to do so by a religion that increasingly ceased to interfere in the province of their business affairs. Preachers in Geneva inveighed against the oppressive use of credit but they were no longer speaking to the reality of the lives of their hearers and, increasingly, they were ignored. The unholy conspiracy has its origins in this separation of religious teaching from business activity.

The separation of education

In another sphere of life in England, higher education was taken away from the monasteries and became separated in the exclusive atmospheres of Oxford and Cambridge. They continued with their emphasis on those subjects which had traditionally been given status in a previous age, and to a large extent ignored the developments in science and technology which the new age of enterprise was bringing. The religion of the Establishment with its culture and social conventions gave a much higher value to classical subjects which would prepare entrants for the professions rather than for a life in industry and commerce. Nonconformists were excluded from these places and were forced to establish their own 'institutes' training people in the skills of their own trade. For these reasons the established church found itself separated from the energies of those who were feeding the life-blood to a vigorous new society. It was the Nonconformists, the Fry's and the Cadbury's and many others who began their own colleges of higher education where a concentration on engineering and science was possible.

Churches in industrial towns

Meanwhile people were teeming into the new industrial towns and they had to find a way of life which would support them in these very different circumstances. The Church of England had its old rural parishes and some clergy did their best to wrestle with the changes which were overtaking them. However, there is little doubt that it was Nonconformity which came closer to giving a Christian ethic to shape lives in industrial Britain. It was in the Methodist, Congregational and Baptist chapels that working men and women found a home and a voice and an opportunity to become responsible for their own religion, and with it their own well-being and their own social and educational betterment.

The Revd Colin McKechnie was a Primitive Methodist minister in the North East of England for forty years from the early 1830s. An account of his life was written by his friend and admirer the Revd John Atkinson and published in 1898. It contained a wonderful, and I am sure typical, account of the atmosphere of a chapel during a miner's strike in the early 1840s. It shows how many of the more able members of the chapel were also leaders in the trades unions and how they were forced to move from their homes as a result of the strike.

Success in church work suffered a serious reverse by what was known for many years, and is even still known, as 'The Great Strike' among the colliers of Durham and Northumberland. The condition of the colliers was not far removed from slavery. They were bound to work in certain collieries for specific periods, their hours of labour were excessive, their wages small, and their general conditions of life poor. With a view to secure an improvement, refused to reasonable appeal, a general strike was organised through the two counties, and continued for some four months or more, entailing much privation and suffering. As the houses in which the colliers lived belonged to the masters, they were evicted wholesale, and with their famil-ies turned out upon the highways. The effect of this strike was disastrous to the churches, for after a lengthened conflict the men had to yield, cold and want fought on the masters' side; and when the collieries were opened again the men who had taken an active part in the strike were refused employment. Most of these men were officials in our churches, and were compelled to migrate or seek other means of gaining a livelihood. Religion had done much in the colliery villages in awakening a sense of manhood which made the servitude, in which they were bound galling to many, and they sought by combination to improve their condition, and though the immediate result was failure, yet out of the struggle, so replete with privation and suffering, there has sprung the unionism which has done so much for the temporal welfare of the coal-miners. Most of the societies in the Newcastle circuit outside the town were shattered and broken, and most of the principal officials banished. It was sad to see the work of years wrecked, and yet who could blame the men for seeking better conditions of life? Certainly not the preachers who had been largely the means of creating the ideals which led the men to aspire to greater freedom and comfort in life. During this time of conflict and distress, while Mr McKechnie took no active part in the dispute between the masters and their workmen, he, along with his colleagues, mixed much with the sufferers, endeavouring in every possible way to comfort, guide, and sustain them in their trying circumstances. It was long, however, before our Northern churches recovered from the effects of this disastrous struggle.[3]

An attempt at analysis

We are extremely fortunate to have another Christian 'classic' which charts the attempts which the churches made to minister to working people in the city of Sheffield. E. R. 'Ted' Wickham's *Church and people in an industrial city*[4] was first published in 1957 and is an extremely competent piece of sociological writing undertaken at a time when there were few in England capable of making connections between the data of the sociologists and the practice of religion. Wickham charts the valiant efforts of the churches from the eighteenth century through to the middle of the twentieth century in their attempts to attract, seat and evangelise working people. In eloquent and persuasive language he charts the failure of attempt after attempt to bring lasting renewal and shows in his forcible way the lack of any discernible ecclesiastical strategy which would try to speak to and understand the values of an industrialised society. He ends his book with despairingly accurate conclusions which are borne out by our experience as well as by the evidence of the statistics themselves:

> *The Church has no policy except that of maintenance*; there is no attempt to work out the required shape of the local church if it is to be a missionary instrument, as distinct from a centre for public worship. And let us have no doubt that a missionary structure has to be planned and organized. There will always be outstanding men who can produce a missionary parish with the bricks to hand, even in the midst of ruin, but the Church cannot hope to man

every parish with outstanding men. This surely is the point of a missionary policy, structure and organization, and a theological training of ministers to serve it — for ordinary mortals can operate a good system, but only extraordinary ones can work effectively in a bad one.

Some of the finest contemporary expressions of mission have been done before on a large scale, and yet have fallen away into desuetude. Thus Sheffield had over a thousand 'district visitors' up to the 'twenties, and, as we have already seen, a vigorous parish like St Mary's, Bramall Lane, had fifty lay workers visiting in the parish, cottage-meetings, and regular visiting of the small local works, at the end of the last century. And yet it all fell away. True, many factors, as we have seen, were responsible; but nonetheless it shows that the missionary character of the local church was a matter of chance, not part of official policy, not built into the very structure of the Church.

Whatever the inside shape of the church — and here there is bound to be diversity of opinion reflecting differences of theology and church order — the case for an outward shape designed for missionary engagement is unanswerable. But it must be based upon over-all persistent policy, largely sustained by the laity and not subject to interruption and new beginning on different lines every three or seven years as ministers come and go.[4]

A faulty seam

Why did the churches not grasp and keep those who shaped this new industrial culture? Is it just that Christianity is always at least a generation behind any social and scientific changes which emerge and only needs time to catch up? Or is there something much deeper? Is there a faulty seam manifesting itself in a conspiracy of silence which runs through the fabric of our national life which envelops the churches and prevents them taking lasting initiatives even when clear opportunities for growth and co-operation present themselves. The next chapters will chart attempts, both crude and sophisticated, to challenge or frustrate the conspirators. We shall then go on to explore what from this history of Christian thought and activity can be of use in our working lives today.

Chapter Three

Track Layers and bridge builders

When a group of apprentices in a Sheffield steelworks discuss trial marriages they describe the arrangement as 'over the brush', a new phrase to the industrial chaplain talking to them. Terry Coleman in *The Railways Navvies* describes marriage in one Navvy community in this way, 'At Woodhead in 1845, where 1,000 men were encamped in shanty huts, they even had their own marriage ceremony; the couple jumped over a broomstick, in the presence of a roomful of men assembled to drink upon the occasion ... they were heathens in a Christian country.'[1] With this description of one social institution a century and a half of industrialisation is spanned by some phrases, such as 'over the brush', transmitted directly through a certain sub-culture. In that same century and a half is spanned the churches' concern about industrialisation and their concern for the people, who almost by the very nature of their occupations, are separated from organised religion and sometimes from Christianity itself.

This separation became the concern of small groups or of individuals within the Christian churches. A look into the origins of their work begins with the development of large industrial communities in the second quarter of the nineteenth century. More particularly it begins with the development of canals and then the railway systems which made industrialisation possible.

Work camp missioners

Canals, railways and then dams were built by gangs of men who travelled from contract to contract wherever new works were beginning. The navigators or 'navvies' as they were called came first from the bankers, the fenmen of Lincolnshire who had built the sea walls, and later from gangs of English and Irish who took up this migrant life. Navvies were not ordinary labourers, though a labourer could become a navvy. Entry qualifications were high. First a man had to be able to withstand the rigours of the work, secondly he had to live in the vast encampments by the lines, thirdly he had to eat and drink like a navvy — two pounds of beef and a gallon of beer a day. This isolation is brought out well by Dick Sullivan in his book *Navvyman*[2]:

> Eighty per cent were English, most of their work was in England, yet they lived like aliens in their own country, often outside its laws, usually outside its national sense of community. They were their own country's non-belongers ... Often they were nameless, known to each other only at second-hand by a nickname. They were a homeless, wandering itinerant people belonging nowhere except to the island as a whole.

At first isolated individuals carried out mission work with the navvies. Some were ordained like James Gilkes and William St George Sargeant, two chaplains during the construction of the Lancaster and Carlisle line. Others were laymen such as Thomas Jenour employed as a Reader by the Pastoral Aid Society on the Croydon and Epsom Railway.

A pioneering woman

Undoubtedly the most formidable of the missioners was a woman, Mrs Elizabeth Garnett. She worked for the Navvy Mission which was formed rather late in the history of the work, in 1878, by a close friend of hers, Louis Moule Evans, a Yorkshire incumbent who later became Dean of Ripon. The *Quarterly Letter to Navvies* was her principal mouth- piece for over forty years. She often addressed her readers, or those who had the Quarterly read to them, as 'my dear mates'. This magazine is a fascinating piece of social and industrial history. As well as the friendly but highly moral letter there was also news of contracts which were ending and of where new works were beginning. The back pages contained information about those injured or killed while at work. It is easy to see why the *Quarterly* was looked to with such interest. The highest ever circulation in 1904 ran to 155,000 and at the outbreak of the First World War editions were at 100,000.[3]

The cry of the missioners was both evangelistic and heavily moral in tone. 'The Gospel' had to be proclaimed. It was delivered by missioners and others at open meetings in the navvy encampments or occasionally in huts constructed by the missioners. Conditions on the sites, the heavy drinking, the impermanence of marriage, all conspired to make the message fall on deaf ears though the social care offered made many missioners well loved characters. There seemed to be little concern about the conditions under which the navvies worked and even less questioning about the system of employment which brought these conditions into being.

The Navvy Mission in its structure was a fine example of Victorian Christian good works. It displayed all the righteous fervour of its cause and with it the class and cultural divisions of Victorian society. Dick Sullivan describes it well:

> To the Victorians the Mission was eminently worthy. It listed the Primate among its patrons, as well as the Arch- bishop of York, most of the English bench of Bishops and sundry lords and gentry. No navvy, however, sat on its committee and only one woman ever did: Mrs Garnett. Yet in spite of the male upper classes at the top it was run by women and working men. Missionaries were black-suited,

white-shirted, dark-tied working men who in summer wore straw boaters with a dove of peace badge pinned to the hat band. The whole Society, naturally in Victorian England, was very class-biased and once the navvy swapped his moleskin for semi-broadcloth he crossed into another lonely life. The Navvies he left distrusted him as one of the others: the others refused to accept him as one of them. Ordination — self-betterment by class-hopping — was discouraged.[4]

The evangelical party in the Church of England was aware of some of the social evils of the time. Shaftesbury, Venn and the Clapham Sect of evangelical Christians did a great deal of campaigning over the issues of child and women's labour. However, the great mass of clergymen, especially in the Church of England, remained indifferent to the early effects of industrialisation. This was less so by 1880. The change can be accounted for by a shift in the prevailing mood of theology and a change in the interests of the clergy themselves, particularly in the greatly expanded cities.

Digging deeper

The questioning and intellectual concern over the effects of industrialisation was coming from men like John Malcolm Ludlow, Charles Kingsley, Frederick Denison Maurice, Thomas Hughes and their associates who between 1848 and 1854 formed a group who called themselves Christian Socialists. Maurice began an attack on what he saw as the whole *laissez faire*, competitive, commercialist spirit of his age and did this in the name of theology. People, he insisted, were not, in their true nature as created by God and redeemed by Christ, mere self-contained individuals who were bound to compete with one another. 'Competition' he wrote to Kingsley, 'is put forth as the law of the universe. That is a lie. The time has come for us to declare that it is a lie by word and deed.'[5] The true law of the universe, claimed Maurice, was that mankind is made to live in community — people realise their true nature when they co-operate with one another as children of God and brothers and sisters in Christ.

Maurice was a scholarly and shy academic but one whose concerns were for working people and their education. Like R. H. Tawney nearly a century later he believed education to be the route by which the great majority of the working population could be led to the possibility of making choices which would free them from the imprisoning conditions in which they lived and which would allow them to take a full part in democratic government.

Maurice had been influenced by Ludlow. The two had first met when Ludlow was a barrister at Lincoln's Inn and Maurice was the Chaplain there. Ludlow had grown up in Paris. He had seen the revolution of 1830 and had been influenced by the utopian socialism of Buchez, Blanc and de Lammenais. An accomplished linguist, Ludlow was an expert in law, politics and economics. He was said to have an intellect equal to that of Maurice but he was more practical. His humility made him less forceful than Maurice. Ludlow was in Paris again in 1848 and reported that socialism was a 'real and a very great power which had acquired an unmistakeable hold, not merely on the fancies but on the consciences of the Parisian workmen, and that it must be Christianised or it would shake Christianity to its foundations, precisely because it appealed to the higher and not the lower instincts of the men.'[6]

If Ludlow saw a challenge to Christianity and wanted to Christianise it, Maurice came to socialism through hearing Ludlow and matching what he heard with his own theology. Maurice had been brought up as a Unitarian and, as he says, he knew its creed 'through and through and deliberately rejected it'. His Anglican theology was based on the Incarnation and his profound understanding of the Fatherhood of God and the brotherhood of mankind. Almost all of Maurice's social thinking is found in embryo in his early *The*

Kingdom of Christ published in 1838 and is developed in *Politics for the people* (1848) and *Christian Socialist* (1850).

Christian Socialism?

The title Christian Socialist, adopted to 'commit us at once to the conflict which we must engage in sooner or later with the unsocial Christians and the unchristian Socialists', did not come until 1850. In his biography of Maurice, C. F. G. Masterman says the name was 'apparently adopted with a desire to offend the maximum number of persons on both sides'.

To what extent was Maurice a socialist? Edward Norman in *Church and Society in England 1770–1970* says of Maurice and his circle that 'their concern for the conditions of the working men was like that of most old-fashioned paternalist clergy who hated the middle-class manufacturers and the industrial England they had created'.[7] Maurice's primary concern was for the education of working men so that they could free themselves from the trap which held them. It appears that when Maurice used the word socialist it was certainly in the sense of the brotherhood of mankind and grew from a reaction to the rampant individualism which he thought industrialisation and commercialism had created. The way in which he applied this sense of brotherhood to political affairs was less than might be understood from the socialism of the French Revolution. His thought was moral rather than economic and his interpretation of socialism was more the encouragement of small-scale co-operative ventures than in the development of any kind of state socialism.

As a theologian Maurice could bring a Christian critique to any institution or movement. He was certainly not an uncritical democratic socialist. When Abraham Lincoln was assassinated in 1865, and some of Maurice's friends were speaking of him as a kind of martyr to democracy, he wrote to Ludlow warning that the virtue of any system of government was in the way it was used, 'I believe the Sovereign has been great in so far as he or she has confessed a ministry — ignominious so far as he or she has clutched at dominion; that the nobles have been great so far as they have confessed a ministry — ignominious in so far as they have been aristocrats or oligarchs. I apply the same maxim to the larger class. If they will accept the franchise as a ministry, be it as high as it may, as a calling, I shall rejoice. If they grasp at any power merely as a power, I believe the voice of Demos will be the devil's voice and not God's.'[8]

In 1853 Maurice was dismissed from the Chair of Divinity at King's College, London, not for his socialism but for his liberal views on eternal punishment. The Council at King's thought that the opinions set out in his book of *Theological Essays* were 'of dangerous tendency and calculated to unsettle the minds of the students at King's College'. In 1854 Maurice founded the Working Men's College in Red Lion Square where he tried to put into practice many of the ideas which he and his colleagues had developed. He went to Cambridge as a professor in 1866.

The influence of this group of men was considerable. Their activities in attempts to provide education for working men had an influence far wider than the confines of the church. Within the church their writings were seminal on a newly developing strand of Christian social thinking which was in fact very different from the benevolent paternalism which characterised much of the social work of the Victorian Church. Outside the church Maurice's ideas were formative in the development of experiments in adult education. There is still a Working Men's College in Crowndale Road, Camden Town in London.

We have been accustomed by church historians to think that the Tractarian and Oxford Movements had the greater influence on ecclesiastical life in mid-nineteenth century. In a little known piece of writing Dr Alec Vidler gives his estimate of the contribution of the Christian Socialists.[9]

I should say that there was a contemporary of the Tractarians who saw more deeply into their discovery of the Church than they did themselves. I mean Frederick Denison Maurice, whose book *The Kingdom of Christ, or Hints on the Principals, Ordinances, and Constitution of the Catholic Church* was published in 1838. There is more to be learned from him about the nature of the Church than all the *Tracts* put together. After first being attracted, Maurice was finally repelled from Tractariansim. He perceived that the error of the Tractarians consisted, as he said, 'in opposing to the spirit of the present age the spirit of a former age, instead of the ever-living and active spirit of God'. He was a Catholic theologian in a larger sense than any of the writers of the *Tracts*.

Here is the truly prophetic voice of Maurice. It was a voice which went unheard for in fact Christian Socialists of succeeding generations did mark 'the spirit of a former age' and replaced Maurice's socialism with their own Guild Socialism.

By 1854 the first phase of what was called the Christian Socialist movement had come to an end. From then until 1877 there was no organised group within the Church of England which concerned itself with the social implications of the gospel. However, the seeds of social concern which had been sown by Maurice and his colleagues were germinating in the lives and activities of a wide variety of clergy and academics.

There were two other movements in later Victorian England which took up the torch of this social concern about the values inherent in industrial societies. They were the Guild of St Matthew and the Christian Social Union.

Steward Headlam and the Guild of St Matthew

Stewart Headlam was a curate of St Matthew Bethnal Green. His flamboyant ways and extreme views drew attention to his activities all too readily. He did however, in his refined and upper-class way, have a clear grasp of what socialism was coming to be about and wanted to claim it for Christianity through the activities and publications of his Guild of St Matthew. He stood as a Fabian socialist and became a member of the London County Council in 1888. In his socialism he had a high view of the state and was optimistic about its possibilities for reforming society. He was a political evangelist who saw, quite rightly, that there existed a struggle between groups in society over the basic assumptions or values upon which a nation should be organised. He believed that there was to be a political — but not a revolutionary — struggle for the control of state power. He saw this power as the instrument for the creation of social justice.

Stewart Headlam was in the new High Anglican Tractarian or Catholic tradition. His socialism came from secular sources like the Fabian Society as much as from his theology. His systematic socialism was well thought out and in some things his views were very advanced. He was a strong advocate for the abolition of private property.

There was some truth in Maurice's criticism of the Tractarians when applied to Headlam also. There was an element of the Guild Socialism, the association of small craft groups, in his thinking. Although his socialism was real enough it contrasted with his extravagant way of life and with the medievalist views of his associates Percy Dearmer and Conrad Noel who were certainly bent on 'opposing the spirit of the age'.

Headlam did succeed in demonstrating that systematic socialism and Christianity were not irreconcilable. In 1884 the Guild approved a thoroughgoing state socialism and passed a resolution which urged all churchmen to support measures which would tend 'to restore to the people the value they give to the land, to bring about a better distribution of the wealth created by labour, to give to the whole body of the people a voice in their own government and to abolish false standards of worth and dignity.'

Headlam believed, as did Maurice, that reform could come through the education of working people. He was a speaker at 'Labour Churches' — the secular societies for working men begun by John Trevor in 1891 and associated with the emerging Labour Party. His concept of socialism was based on his understanding of Christ which he described in his Fabian Tract, No 42, on Christian Socialism published in 1892. In this he linked his high view of the state to his high view of the Church which he saw as 'mainly and chiefly for doing on a large scale throughout the world those secular, socialistic, works which Christ did on a small scale in Palestine'. Nonetheless, compared with other socialist movements of its time the Guild of St Matthew looked and was rather eccentric. It was not geared to understand or address the shapers of industry and commerce of its time. It was too attracted to medievalism and to the idea of Guild Socialism rather than to the politics of those inside or outside the church.

Scott-Holland the the Christian Social Union

The Christian Social Union was more attractive, more moderate in its views, more academically respectable and altogether more within the Church of England. Founded in 1889 by Henry Scott-Holland, then a Canon of St Paul's, this very different kind of organisation requires careful scrutiny since it had a large influence on many academics and clergy who were to become leaders of the Anglican church in the first forty years of the twentieth century.

B. F. Westcott, Bishop of Durham and formerly Regius Professor of Theology at Cambridge, was its first President. Charles Gore, theologian, co-founder of the Community of the Resurrection and later Bishop of Oxford was an enthusiastic supporter. A leaflet was issued to announce the establishment of the new society.

This Union consists of churchmen who have the following objects at heart:
— To claim for the Christian Law the ultimate authority to
  rule social practice.
— To study in common how to apply the moral truths and
  principles of Christianity to the social and economic
  difficulties of the present time.
— To present Christ in practical life as the Living Master
  and King, the enemy of wrong and selfishness, the power
  of righteousness and love.

One of the first actions of the C.S.U. was to become
associated with Cardinal Manning and his attempt with
others to settle the Dock Strike in 1889. The new organisation grew rapidly and adopted a campaigning style. It
started 'white lists' in various towns of trades-people who
were deserving of custom because they were responsible
employers. C.S.U. members investigated and published
instances of overwork, bullying and beggarly wages and
went into facts about phosphorous poisoning, lead poisoning
and accidents from unguarded machines. The Union also
tried to improve conditions under which women were
employed. By 1895 the C.S.U had twenty-seven branches
with a membership of more than 2,600. The Annual Report
of the Oxford branch for that year reported that it 'had
published six pamphlets and seventeen leaflets. Considerable
practical results have followed from the action of the Branch
in regard to the conditions of work in various local trades'.

The journal of the C.S.U. was called *Commonwealth*. It
was an influential booklet which Scott-Holland edited, and
to which he was the principal contributor. Stephen Paget, his
biographer, says that in *Commonwealth* he could be, when
he was at his best, 'genius in its shirtsleeves'.

A pamphlet issued at the inauguration of the C.S.U. bears
the marks of Scott-Holland's writing and illustrates the
importance the Union gave to the influence of industry on
society.

45

We believe that political problems are rapidly giving place to the industrial problem, which is proving itself more and more to be the question of the hour. It is the condition of industry which is absorbing all attention and all anxieties. It is the needs and necessities of industry which are the motive powers now at work to mould and direct the fortunes of human society. It is the intolerable situation in which our industrial population now finds itself, that must force upon us a reconsideration of the economic principles and methods which have such disastrous and terrible results . . .

Here is a clear recognition of the major influence which industry was having on the lives of the people of Britain and an attempt by a group of churchmen to examine and challenge the values which they saw inherent in industrialisation. There was no cry for a retreat back to a nostalgic medievalism but a right challenge to the values which were the motive forces for rampant industrial growth and the often cruel individualism which went with it.

Scott-Holland was aware that there was a gulf between Christian morality and economic theory and that there had been little thinking done either to build a bridge or to develop integrated theories. He wrote a preface to the published Sion College lectures of 1890 which were given by Canon Richmond and entitled *Economic morals*.

The scraps of economic philosophy which most of us have picked up belong to that political economy which, in the days of our youth, was still in the condition of an isolated science. . . .The gap between the isolated laws which these catch phrases signalise, and the actual living world with which we are dealing is immense. . . .We live as shuttlecocks, bandied about between our political economy and our Christian morality. We go a certain distance with the science, and then, when things get ugly and squeeze, we suddenly introduce moral considerations, and human kindness, and charity. And then, again, this seems weak, and we pull up short and go back to tough economic principle. So we live in miserable double-mindedness. . . .There is thus no consistency in our treatment of facts; no harmony in our inward convictions.

How was any kind of harmony in our inward convictions to be developed? Many of the C.S.U. leaders, especially Scott-Holland and Gore, had been members of a group of Oxford theologians who produced in 1889 a book of what at the time seemed to be controversial essays called *Lux Mundi*. These scholars were both Catholic and Modernist and wished to revise Christian thinking within the Anglican tradition because, as Gore said in his Preface, theology has to develop 'in the light of new social and intellectual movements'.

'Lux Mundi' and a theology of Incarnation

What was this theology which they sought to develop? It was based firmly on the Incarnation, as Gore described it, 'Christianity is faith in a certain person Jesus Christ'. In the person of Jesus they saw the manifestation of God and the revelation of true man. Arguments for the development of a new scheme of social ethics were based on this fundamental understanding of the way in which the Son of God had taken upon himself human nature. Arthur Lyttelton in his essay on the Atonement says:

> It has been the fault of much popular theology to think only of our deliverance from wrath by the sacrificial death of Christ, and to neglect the infinitely important continuation of the process thus begun. The Gospel is a religion of life, the call to a life of union with God by means of the grace which flows from the mediation of the risen and ascended Saviour.[10]

Many of the *Lux Mundi* group were influenced also by the English Idealist School of philosophy led by T. H. Green. Scott-Holland had been Green's pupil and friend while at Oxford and was attracted to the kind of ethical thinking

47

which was systematic and inclusive and which was a reaction to the empiricism of Hume and the utilitarianism of Mill.[11]

Why was the C.S.U. so influential, particularly with many who were to become leaders in the Anglican Church? It may well be that openminded clergy saw in the activities of the C.S.U. a way of addressing the same secular problems their contemporaries in other professions had to face. There was also a natural outworking of concern for social problems which arose from very much more concerned parochial clergy. In addition many academics and future church leaders had been given a taste of life in poor areas through the University Settlement movement. A look at the list of names of future distinguished men who worked at Oxford House in Bethnal Green illustrates this well. The C.S.U. provided a vehicle by which these men could think through the implications of what they had witnessed of poverty and inner-city life.

The Great War of 1914–18 forced a great divide in Christian thinking as well as in almost every other part of British life. The one figure who brought wider influence to British theology both before and after the war was Charles Gore. More needs to be said about the man and the theology which he represented.

The influence of Charles Gore

Charles Gore was the kind of churchman who does not exist today. He had a powerful intellect and a commanding personality. He combined a lifelong dedication to ecclesiastical affairs with a broad interest in international politics and in social and industrial questions of concern to Britain. Above all, he was a theologian who always encouraged his associates, whether ordinands, fellow academics or national leaders not to leap to solutions before explaining the fundamental principles underlying an issue. He always described himself as a free thinker though none of his discussions led him away from the Christian faith.

That faith is described as Liberal Catholic. It drew from the scriptures and from the tradition of the Church in order to determine the will of God in contemporary events. It was a working-out of Gore's understanding of the Incarnation which was explored in *Lux Mundi*.

In the same year that the essays were published he became, with Scott-Holland, one of the founder Vice Presidents of the C.S.U. While he was Principal of Pusey House it was Gore's Oxford branch which carried out detailed investigations into local conditions of employment. After a brief time as Vicar of the small Oxfordshire village of Radley in 1893 he became a residentiary Canon of Westminster Abbey. Here he secured a base and a wider following for his biblical teaching and his social concern.

'Lord Salisbury's surprise', as Gore's appointment as Bishop of Worcester was called, is certainly an argument for the retention of Crown influence in ecclesiastical appointments. Salisbury saw that there was a divorce of religious leadership in the Church of England from its episcopate. He was far from approving Gore's opinions, but was determined to recommend him to the Crown as a leader of great influence.[12]

Although Gore's social theology was in the tradition of Maurice, he said in an interview towards the end of his life that the turning point in his life had been a tour of the Oxfordshire villages in the company of Joseph Arch, and that the writings of Maurice, for whom he had a profound respect, had played a minor part.[13] While not directly following Maurice, Gore's incarnational theology certainly had echoes of Maurice's. It probably came to Gore through the influence of Westcott and perhaps also through the influence of Stewart Headlam who first brought together the theology of Maurice and Tractarian churchmanship.

Gore, Scott-Holland and their associates influenced Christian social thought for a span of forty years. It is the result of that influence which will introduce us to facets of English church life in the early twentieth century.

Taking the message into the churches

In 1906 a joint committee of Convocation and the House of Laymen was appointed by the Representative Church Council to report on the moral witness which the Church ought to bear on economic questions. The committee produced a report in 1907 largely drafted by Gore. Its main recommendation has a remarkably contemporary ring. The Christian moral duty to love one's neighbour as oneself meant that no one should regard another person as a mere instrument for his own advantage; the other's interest and well-being demanded equal consideration. Moreover, a special deference was due to the helpless and weak.[14]

As the outcome of this report, Convocation pressed the desirability of forming in every diocese, as part of local Church organisation, a Standing Social Service Committee. Gore thought that this was the official recognition by the Church of the methods adopted by the C.S.U. He wanted to resign as President and after a serious internal debate only continued until the middle of 1911. He saw these diocesan committees as the channel through which the efforts of the C.S.U. should now flow. New methods were required and new people to operate them.

The second report to which Gore contributed and which set the tone for social action in the 1920s was the committee on Christianity and Industrial Problems which arose from the National Mission of Repentance and Hope of 1916. The Report embodied principles which Gore had advocated and for which he had contended for many years. It based all economic arrangements on the foundation of moral premises, and claimed that the economic process must submit and conform to Christian principles, so far as to impose the living

wage, together with adequate leisure and security of employment, as a first charge on industry, recognise the responsible
status of the worker within his own trade, and provide full
opportunities for all in education, health and housing.[15]

It was largely to enable these proposals to be strengthened
that a new organisation was formed in 1919. As Maurice
Reckitt says, the Industrial Christian Fellowship came into
being as a timely fusion of an evangelistic agency (the Navvy
Mission) which lacked a social message, and a 'socially
minded' organisation (the C.S.U.) which had never achieved
any contact with the working class.[16] It is with the establishment of the I.C.F. that a new chapter begins. With the death
of Scott-Holland in 1918 so too a new generation was to
come into prominence.

Chapter Four

Between the Wars

The twentieth century has sealed the separation of church and society in the everyday lives of the majority of the population. There is a similar actual divide in our civic and commercial life, though on public occasions an uneasy truce is maintained. This was brought home most forcefully to me when I read an anecdote which Archbishop William Temple used in his *Christianity and Social Order*[1] first published in 1942. Here he tells the story of a group of bishops who attempted to bring government, coal owners and miners together to try to settle the Coal Strike of 1926. Apparently the reply they got from the Prime Minister, Stanley Baldwin, asked the bishops how they would like it if the Iron and Steel Federation offered to revise the Athanasian Creed! The reply was claimed as a legitimate score.

The Archbishop went on at the beginning of his first chapter to say it was assumed that the Church exercised little influence upon society, that it ought to exercise none, and that this assumption had always been made by reasonable people. He went on to build an historical argument for church intervention on social questions and followed this with a method for the Church to make its presence felt.

The divide of the Great War

The first half of this century, in which Temple played so large a part in the Christian discussion of social issues, was a time when Christians recognised the scale of the divide and tried to devise strategies by which to bridge it. The springboard for new thinking and action was the Great War of 1914–18. It took many of the nations of Europe through a vale of turmoil and suffering and brought them to new ground where so many terrible experiences had to be evaluated and understood. The land to which troops returned was not fit for heroes and some were quick to challenge assumptions about life as they had known it before the War.

Many of the best clergy in Britain had become Forces' chaplains. Their closeness to ordinary working people had been as much a revelation to them as had been their exposure to such awful conditions. During the War, in 1916, there had been the National Mission of Repentance and Hope which was an attempt to recall Britain to Christian values. It did not meet with any great success and was tinged with patriotism. After the war a study was undertaken on Christian belief and people's reactions to the experience of the War. In 1918 a group of clergy and laymen was convened by the Young Men's Christian Association (Y.M.C.A.) to look at the effects of the war on religious attitudes. Their report was published in a book called *The Army and Religion*[2]. It is full of fascinating comments by servicemen about their beliefs.

In the section on 'Misunderstandings' some of the comments have a very modern ring. From a Corporal in the R.F.A., 'The general idea of Christianity is that it consists of a number of negative commandments. This is more or less aided by military discipline, which in France is one long series of "Thou shalt not"s. By this I do not wish to infer that soldiers do not do any good actions, that would be untrue, but it is generally regarded as doing the straight thing, not so much a good turn, and to suggest it was a Christian act would be instantly denied.'

From a Private in the R.A.M.C., 'Their idea of a Christian life is greatly at fault. To them a Christian is a Church-goer, a man who prays, who reads his Bible and generally lives a meek inoffensive sort of life and believes he goes to Heaven when he dies. To the man who has this idea of a Christian it means a life with all pleasure, pure and otherwise, crossed out with the words, "Thou shalt not".'

What radiates from that book over and above all the documentation of belief or confusion is the rediscovery of a vital new faith *by the chaplains themselves*. They too returned to homes and parishes changed by the experience. Many of them were very much the better as parish clergy after the war. Some felt that the comparative tranquillity of parish and congregational life was not sufficient either for themselves or for the future of the church. There needed to be the sharpness of social action and of mission to continue to 'engage' with working people and for the church to continue to work out its theology in the aftermath of war.

The Industrial Christian Fellowship

One of the most significant organisations for mission and for contact with working people in these years was founded in 1919. At the end of the last chapter we saw that the Industrial Christian Fellowship emerged from the amalgamation of the rather reflective Christian Social Union and the more evangelistic Navvy Mission. The I.C.F. as it has always been known developed rapidly and gained significant national influence. It had bishops and industrialists to form its council, with a national secretary and 'messengers', some with local and others with national responsibility.

The most significant of the national messengers in the 1920s was Geoffrey Studdert Kennedy. He had gained considerable fame and prominence during the War as an army chaplain. He had the nickname 'Woodbine Willie' from the packets of Wills Woodbines cigarettes the chaplains were issued with to give out to the troops. He was a close friend of the Revd Dick Sheppard who after the war, was vicar of St Martin-in-the Fields, Trafalgar Square, and William Temple who was rector of St James', Picadilly. 'Tubby' Clayton was a member of this same group and was encouraged by them to begin the Toc H fellowship movement for ex-service men. Studdert Kennedy was already well known as a popular preacher and as the author of collections of verse or collo-quial rhymes.[3] In these he tried to articulate the human, folk and religious feelings of soldiers and of ordinary people. He first took a parish in Worcester and then came to London as Vicar of St Edmund the King and Martyr in Lombard Street. During this time he worked for the I.C.F. conducting preach-ing missions in factories and at factory gates. He invited many of his friends to join him. In Iremonger's biography of William Temple[4] there is a typical picture of the Archbishop in an overhead crane operator's cabin preaching to several hundred assembled workers at the British Thomson-Houston works in Rugby.

I.C.F.'s anchor-man was its General Secretary, Prebendary P.T.R. Kirk. It was he who developed the national organis-ation with secretaries and messengers across the country. At first glance it seems that the I.C.F. had many influential friends in industry, commerce and government and that these were won simply through the vigour of the organisation and because many of its leading supporters shared a common social background — William Temple and R. H. Tawney shared the same train when they went to Rugby School together as new boys. Dick Sheppard's social contacts and influence were enormous. It is sufficient for my conspiracy theory that the I.C.F was an organisation which attempted through its Christian social thinking and action to bridge a gulf which already existed between the Christian faith and the real opinion-formers in society.

In doing this alone the I.C.F. attracted controversy as well as support. I have already repeated the anecdote of the bishops and the Coal owners. Theologians also were critical of Studdert Kennedy's preaching which demolished the triumphalism of Victorian and Edwardian religion and went, so they would say, close to the heresy of suggesting that God suffered with his people. Controversial as this may have been, there was a need for a theology which took seriously and grappled with, first of all a horrific war, and then mass unemployment and a General Strike. The I:C.F. preached to these issues and wrote about them. The *Quarterly*, continued from the Navvy Mission, makes interesting social and theological reading as it continued through these years to discuss important social issues through the eyes of many national figures. Interestingly, the *Quarterly* continues to be published to this day and many opinions developed in this book first saw the light of day between its slim covers.

The I.C.F. undermined?

More controversially Dr Peter Sedgwick in an article, 'Not ceasing from exploring'[5] published in 1987 for the Church of England Board for Social Responsibility, has suggested that the I.C.F. was either duped or was a willing partner in a much more suspect conspiracy. Sedgwick suggests that from 1916 onwards the British Civil Service began to see its role in government as bringing a much stronger sense of continuity to political life. It began to attempt to bring to an end the system of strongly adversarial politics where policies were considerably changed when the political colour of the government changed. He maintains that 'consensus politics' came to be the result of this strengthening of the position of the Civil Service. We might say that the scripts for the television series 'Yes Minister' began to be written here!

Sedgwick draws into his argument Christian leaders and the I.C.F. In what he says he is supported by a critical analysis of the work of the I.C.F. and Geoffrey Studdert Kennedy in *Dog Collar Democracy*[6] written by Gerald Studdert Kennedy, a nephew of the I.C.F.'s Messenger and published in 1982. His argument is that by the middle of the First World War a group of intellectuals and politicians abandoned hope in political democracy and saw the future for Britain in a more paternalistic form of government with a new structure of relationships between the state and the economic and social order.

In order to achieve this there had to be stronger coalition formed between business and politics. The aim was to reduce industrial and political conflict at the expense of a higher view of the State. The younger Studdert Kennedy argues that I.C.F. and its supporters were, willingly or unwittingly, recruited, to this campaign. He illustrates his argument with examples commending corporate intervention from the writings of William Temple and the sermons of Geoffrey Studdert Kennedy.

It is difficult to decide whether or not there was such a concerted ideological campaign, and if the I.C.F. was recruited into it. What is certain is that there was a growing sense that there should be State, corporate, responsibility for social welfare and that there should be increasing government intervention in more and more avenues of national life. Such a policy was encouraged by William Temple and his followers. They did think that social change could be brought about, and the weak protected, if they could influence the rich and the powerful. Consequently there was a deliberate effort to recruit Christian sympathisers into the I.C.F.'s activities and to involve them in its major conferences.

C.O.P.E.C. and Malvern

There were two national conferences in the heyday of the I.C.F. about Christianity and national, political and industrial questions. In 1924 a conference was held in Birmingham on a scale never before attempted. It was known as C.O.P.E.C. ('Conference on Christian Politics, Economics and Citizenship). Temple, by this time Bishop of Manchester, was chairman. It is through his influence that the proceedings of the conference were held together in a coherent way. The Commission reports fill twelve weighty volumes. The 1,500 delegates, eighty from overseas, were convinced that the way to combat the most serious problems, economic and social, of their day was with corporate Christian action. Good systematic thinking, informed by the best minds in the country, should be brought to bear on our most pressing national problems. Solutions on policies should then be presented and Christian laymen and others be encouraged to pursue reforms in the real but messy world of politics, including commerce and social welfare. Alongside principles established went the concept of 'middle axioms' which were working hypotheses which allowed compromise and negotiation as policies were pursued.

The Malvern Conference is the other great landmark in the Christian social policy making of the time. In 1941 the I.C.F., through the influence of P.T.R. Kirk, drew together by invitation 400 businessmen, economists, theologians and sociologists to begin to think about economic and social reconstruction once the war was over. Kirk managed to persuade Temple, now Archbishop of York, to be Chairman. The conference stumbled over several days and almost broke up in disarray. On the final morning Temple produced a series of 'conclusions' which he asked the much relieved Conference to approve. Most were sound and gave great heart to those still trying to bring about reconstruction through consensus politics. Malvern also saw 'stumbling blocks' which made it harder for people to live fully Christian lives. The private ownership of the principal industrial resources was seen as one of these. Some politicians say that it was the fruit of such thinking which was seen in government policies from 1944 onwards in the areas of education, health and welfare and in the limitation of industrial ownership.

The real conspiracy re-emerges

Attractive or subversive as the Sedgwick/Studdert Kennedy argument is, it seems to me that a reading of Tawney's

Religion and the Rise of Capitalism or Temple's *Christianity and Social Order* places the motives elsewhere. They are as I describe them in the previous chapter in a reading of the history of the late Middle Ages, of the sixteenth and seventeenth centuries where, quite deliberately, businessmen excluded the thinking of the churches from their affairs. The churches colluded with this, preferring, at best to develop only a personal, private code of ethical behaviour.

A look at the proceedings of C.O.P.E.C. and the Malvern Conference[7] shows considerable analysis of economic questions with some of the very best minds of the day making contributions. Where solutions are offered there is still a harking back to the medieval ideal of a form of guild socialism for craftsmen and, at this time, an acceptance of the possibility of stronger central authority. The high view of the State does exist and with it a much greater will to intervene in education, health-care and industrial relations. It is possible to trace directly the establishment of state education through the Butler Act of 1944, the development of the Welfare State following the Beveridge Report and other social legislation to thinking which stems from this corporatist movement. For me these years are the high-water mark of Church-State collaborative thinking in this century. The results of this dialogue are shown in the political and social liberal consensus which was maintained in the years after the Second World War.

The most significant question to follow from all this is, if the Church had attained such a high degree of influence, why and how did it slip away so rapidly? It was not only the death of William Temple in 1944 that brought this about. It was a lack of systematic thinking by church people and an unhealthy interest in, and concern for, internal order questions at the expense of a concern for the social and technical events which were reshaping our worlds.

Here my main conspiracy theory emerges again. Instead of the Churches continuing head-on with collaborative working with industry, commerce and the State they allowed these central activities only to be carried on by what have become known as 'specialist ministers' and in doing so have either imagined that the whole of this work was being done or have willingly acquiesced in a continuing comfortable conspiracy.

The specialist ministry which concerns us here is Industrial Mission. It has achieved some outstanding pieces of work and at times has been an influential movement within the churches. However, because those involved in this work have been marginalised by the churches, their wider influence has been muted. The conspiracy is indeed to allow an unholy calm to continue while the decline of our industries continues. Those who could offer solutions remain unwilling to explore the fundamental causes of this decline.

Chapter Five

Industrial Mission: the new frontier

Industrial Mission did not become what it set out to be. It has suffered in the most overt way from the conspiracy theory which I have been developing. Industrial Missioners were like the 'cuckoo in the nest' of industry. They were attempting to develop what the churches claim as their main objective: the training of the laity to be the Church in the world. It was always going to be difficult because Industrial Mission gained the 'inside information' with which to expose the conspiracy. Its chaplains discovered the gap of theory and practice between business and the gospel. They had to be silenced. The story of Industrial Mission is, first of all, of a European movement which was born in the Second World War largely as a result, once again, of the 'identification' which clergy achieved with working people in desperate times. The possibility of success for Industrial Mission became a threat both to established churches and to the conspiracy which the world of commerce and industry enjoyed to keep the values of the Christian religion well away from their worlds of work.

What I am describing here is by no means a history of Industrial Mission but an account of its place in the attempt to reconstruct a bridge between Christian ideas and those of a prevailing and increasingly pluralistic culture. Industrial Mission in the 1940s and 1950s had a number of strands. These differed primarily according to the culture of the European countries in which they were developing. In the more secularised France where there was greater separation between management and workers and a more pronounced strand of communism in the trades unions, the Worker Priest movement began. In England where the consensus movement, possibly established by the Civil Service and encouraged by the churches, was dominant it was possible for chaplains to visit people at work within factories. While in Germany and Holland, where the churches had a stronger financial relationship with the state or where the atmosphere of postwar reconstruction was stronger, conference houses or Laity Centres were established for dialogue about Christianity and the experience of working people.

Worker-Priests in France

The Worker-Priest movement in France was the fruit of impressive research in the 1930s by the sociologist Gabriel le Bras. He surveyed attendance at Mass in the regions of France on their major local festivals. In his analysis of these figures he concluded that it was in the industrialised areas of France that attendance at Mass was at its lowest. Armed with information of this kind his colleagues and friends used 'religious sociology' as a theoretical framework for mission in a France which they saw as secularised by the acids of industrialisation.

In 1940 the Catholic Hierarchy in France set up an enquiry into the methods of training employed in theological seminaries. One consequence of this was that in October 1942 the seminary of the Mission de France was opened in Lisieux. Its purpose was to train priests specifically for ministries in mission areas. After attending a training course at Liseux two Young Christian Worker Chaplains, Henri Godin and Yvan Daniel, suggested to the Bishop of Paris, Cardinal Suhard, that a special kind of city mission with priests freed from ordinary parish duties be established. Their report was published as, *France, Pays de Mission?*, later translated into English by Masie Ward as *France Pagan?*[1] It is a strong and dynamic call for French Catholicism to grasp this newly-perceived evil and attack it with missionary zeal. Even in translation, Godin's informed and forceful writing reads attractively and strongly and makes the writings of William Temple look like the speculations of an amateur, which in this league, they were.

In an heroic part of this movement priests went, dressed as civilian workers, with thousands of others who were being transported to German labour camps. On 1 July 1943 the Abbés Godin and Daniel were commissioned to begin work with the Mission de Paris. Unfortunately Abbé Godin was killed in an accident in 1944 but other priests joined and the work grew. Missions were founded in other parts of France. Priests took secular jobs and lived in ordinary workers' houses or flats.

It was inevitable that, with the prevailing political opinions of workers at that time, the worker-priests moved politically to the left. Many joined trades unions and, because they were both educated and articulate, became Union officials. This caused great concern in the home church and also in the Vatican. Many of the French bishops continued to support the worker-priests and made public declarations in their favour. However, the overt communism of many of the Unions, especially the C.G.T., was bound to cause alarm.

The movement grew and developed an influence out of all proportion to its numbers. Not only had a radical kind of identification been achieved, but also the priests had succeeded in thinking through their situations and quite strategically set out to urge changes in society, changes which challenged the values of the owners and managers of many industries. They also implicitly challenged some of the right wing attitudes of the Catholic church to the societies which helped to create and uphold it. Opposition grew and increasingly heavy demands were being made to the worker-priests to restrict their activities and become more obviously priests associated with the internal structures of their church.

On the 28 December 1953 the Jesuits withdrew their

worker-priests. On the 10 January *Le Monde* published a text by Cardinal Lienart saying that it was impossible to be totally a priest and totally a workman at the same time. On the 19 January all the French bishops with worker-priests in their dioceses met in Paris. They agreed on a letter which should be sent by each Bishop to every worker-priest in his diocese. The conditions for continuation of their work were:

(1) Restriction of manual work to three hours per day.
(2) Prohibition of all 'temporal' commitments.
(3) Return to clerical company and living quarters (presbytery or monastery).
(4) Prohibition on formation of a national (i.e. supra-diocesan) organisation.
(5) The restrictions to take effect from 1 March 1954.

What these restrictions show is a demand for the re-clericalisation of the priests' lives. The demand for only three hours' work per day and for accommodation in presbyteries or monasteries was a way of keeping the priests in their clericalised culture. The effectiveness of their mission lay in their close identification with the issues and concerns of their associates. Much of this would be lost if they were removed from the immediate scenes of their activity and if their full commitment to equal working conditions were surrendered. It was a severe attempt to re-establish the boundaries or 'separate spheres' of activity and thus ensure that the conspiracy was maintained.

Although the 'experiment' was ended and at its height the worker-priest movement numbered little over one hundred, the ripples from this movement were considerable. The worker-priests broke down boundaries and confused social roles. They forced many of the people they met, by their very presence, to look again at the Gospel message which they were trying to embody. The speed of closure of the experiment is a measure of its impact if not of its immediate success. The full story of the rise and fall of the worker-priests is told in *The Church and Industrial Society* by Gregor Siefer.[2]

Theirs is a story of a movement in a Church which has since changed beyond all recognition. The Second Vatican Council took place only ten years after these events. On many social questions, and in particular the relation of work to society, the Roman Catholic Church has a record of interesting and important pronouncements and encyclicals. In later chapters we shall explore some of these attempts to bridge this gap between the values of work and of the Christian faith.

A pen picture of Henri Perrin, one of the worker-priests, serves well to describe the heroism and the emotion caught up in this movement. During the war he had disguised himself as a worker and had gone to Germany with other conscripts. He was discovered and sent home but while there he found that he could exercise his ministry in this very special way.

After the war he worked in a number of small firms in Paris. When the Catholic hierarchy there decided not to allow him to continue he went to work on the construction of the Isère-Arc dam on the river Isère at Notre-Dame-de-Briançon. At the beginning of 1952 he joined the C.G.T. — the communist dominated and largest of the French trades unions. Between then and 1954 he was involved as a leader in two major strikes.

Henri Perrin was killed in a motor-cycle accident before he was able to give us his own account of this worker-priest experiment, or to show how he would respond to the ban on his activities.

The account of his funeral by Georges Hourdin in the Church of St Hippolyte in Paris describes well the wide interpretations of the nature of priesthood in the French Catholic church at the time.[3]

> His Requiem was celebrated on a Saturday morning in the thirteenth *arrondissement*, where he had so many friends,

so that the poor who had known and loved him could gather round him once more. The choir was full of priests in surplices: they, too, had come to pay their colleague a last tribute. Before the absolution the parish priest invited all the clergy present in the church to come forward and take their places round the coffin. We thought he was referring only to the priests in the sanctuary, but to our astonishment we saw men in lay clothes making their way out from among the crowded congregation. They walked up to the coffin: truly a splendid guard of honour. They were the priests of the *Mission Ouvrière de Paris*, of whom some had submitted, others had not yet given up their manual work; about forty of them. They had all turned up. . . .Deep emotion was written on their tense faces. . . .Their unity with the Church was restored for the moment, and we all recited the Our Father together.

That was the last time the *Mission de Paris* met together.

Industrial Mission

At almost the same time as the worker-priests were at their height in France industrial mission was beginning in England. The rather reserved and austere looking Leslie Hunter had become Bishop of Sheffield in 1939. He had been a curate and associate of Dick Sheppard at St Martin-in-the-Fields and a Student Christian Movement chaplain. He had close links with the churches in Europe. Much of the Sheffield diocese, covering what we now call South Yorkshire, was dominated by steel works and coal mines. In 1944, after discussions with employers and the trades unions, he brought the young 'Ted' Wickham from his chaplaincy in the Royal Ordnance Factory in Woolwich to be his chaplain in the Don Valley steelworks of Sheffield.

Wickham was an energetic, forceful character with a ready wit and, often peering over his glasses, a keen debater. He established a pattern of regular visits to steelworks hoping to establish Christian 'cells' but in fact developed a pattern of informal meetings in the natural groupings of shop-floor and office workers. There were similar meetings for managers, mixed meetings and discussions with 'Outward bound' type expeditions to the hills for apprentices. Wickham built up a team of chaplains in South Yorkshire in the 1940s and 1950s, not without some controversy among the parish clergy. Since those times Industrial Missions have been established throughout Britain and, with varying degrees of success, in India, Australia, the U.S.A., and in several African countries.

Phillip Bloy, a Sheffield Chaplain from 1951-60 has written about 'meal-break' meetings which were so much the stock-in-trade of the missioners.

The 'Meal-break' Meetings

The characteristic happening, in many departments where it was feasible, was the 'meal-break' meeting. Such meetings used to take place in a space around someone's job or in the 'snap-cabin' or in the middle of an office or laboratory. An essential feature was that they were visible in such a way that anyone seeing them in progress could stroll over and lend an ear and, if so disposed, join in. Numbers in these groups might range between ten and thirty. The group would be got together not so much by the missioner (though he or she did not hold back idle in the matter) but by a person in the department, someone readily responded to and respected by his mates. He (or perhaps she, in a department mainly of women) was very likely a non church-member, but a person who thought it worthwhile to get 'the lads' to rally round. One such 'convenor' in the bar mill at the former Steel Peech & Tozer, recalled that many were 'cagey' about coming round and being confronted by 'the vicar' but that those who let their arms be twisted found that they enjoyed themselves. The talking was about whatever was most on people's minds, perhaps some contentious item in the national or world news or some industrial relations issue affecting those present. Like any meal-break occasions these were highly informal, with good-humoured banter and argument. We did not necessarily stick to the subject we started on. If some wag more than half-way out on the edge of the group shouted 'how do you believe in the resurrection? . . . No one's ever come back to tell us!', that question could take over the rest of the time! The meetings were necessarily brief; normally twenty minutes (one person reminiscing spoke of night-shift meetings, which contrived to go on longer!). We could not go far with any subject in such a short period. But we never expected to. It wasn't the point. 'The industrial mission in its style of starting discussions made people think' (comment from a worker in Arthur Lee's wire department).

The meal-break meeting was Ted Wickham's device. He employed it from the very beginning (in Firth Vickers Staybrite Works). He was a brilliant exponent of 'between man and man' dialogue, quick and humorous in repartee, adept at pressing theological points in straightforward and stimulating language. This example inspired the missioners who in turn joined him. We found that, even if not possessed of the extra-special talents, we were able to pursue this method. A few lay members in the mission came to use it too. There were indeed certain basic qualifi-cations. First, we had to know the theology of Old Testa-ment prophecy and New Testament gospel in relation to society. Secondly we had to have the capacity to initiate a discussion positively, conclude it pointedly and, in the main part of the meeting, enable others to do much of the talking. And there was the pre-condition always: of finding the best 'contact' person or 'convenor' in the department.[4]

This industrial mission movement became widely known in Britain in the 1950s and 1960s. Many capable men and a few women were drawn in and in most industrial cities established a 'visiting chaplain' style of industrial mission. The Methodist minister Bill Gowland developed similar kind of work in Luton, to which he added a residential conference centre, the Luton Industrial College. The Church of Scotland pioneered similar work through the Revd George Wilkie.

The Church of England produced a report, *The Task of the Church in Relation to Industry*[5] with Wickham as secretary in 1959. It outlined a strategy for the development of industrial mission across England which would have taken seriously the attack on the values of many in industry and commerce. There was also a nod to the agricultural industry. However, the conspiracy of Church and Society was too great to allow these recommendations to develop. Wickham understood this and had been researching this very separation himself.

In 1957 he published *Church and People in an Industrial City.*[6] In this he interpreted church attendance and church building figures in Sheffield from the late eighteenth century to the beginning of this. Wickham concluded that the decline in church life and church attendance was directly related to the expansion of industrial towns and cities. Of particular interest to his generation was the conclusion that the Church of England had not lost the industrialised working classes — it never had them. Today these conclusions seem almost commonplace but in the 1960s they were seen to give a historical/sociological perspective, not to say explanation, about the dramatic decline in church attendance in the twentieth century. Wickham's flowing style, and his then radical conclusions, gave colour to his work as did his persuasive, often called prophetic, style when he was given an audience for his ideas.

Was *Church and People* unfolding the conspiracy theory? Wickham's conclusions were based on empirical evidence and the weight of his argument was placed on attendance and seating provision figures. With nearly forty years of hindsight the book, which many of my generation thought was etched in stainless steel, has tarnished. The statistical evidence for Sheffield cannot be uniformly applied throughout the country. Later studies have shown the rapid expansion of Catholicism, a revival of Anglican attendance towards the end of the nineteenth century and a flourishing of Nonconformity at the height of the Industrial Revolution.[7]

Nevertheless, Wickham's conclusions with particular regard to English working class communities does stand the test of time if only because the English rural workers, unlike the Irish, the Scottish and the Welsh, came from a culture which had already failed to Christianise them. The conspiracy was already in place and could not be unlocked.

The decline of the influence of industrial missioners

The decline and failure of effective industrial mission on Wickham's terms has its cause elsewhere. Superficially it was thought to have its weakness in the over-clericalisation of the movement but gradually it has become apparent that the movement's momentum was lost when the increasingly 'liberal' consensus politics of the previous fifty years began to crumble.

It was an American, the Revd Scott Paradise, a former Sheffield chaplain who described this break-down most graphically in the middle-class Episcopalian churches of the Eastern Seaboard of the U.S.A. The situation he described was very similar for us in England in the 1970s and 1980s. He wrote an Audenshaw paper in 1974 called, *Requiem for American Industrial Missions.*[2] He describes the breakdown of a consensus which allowed the conspiracy theory to flourish and the resulting polarisation of attitudes. Missioners chose to take a stance which, though with a high moral tone, would lead to their eventual marginalisation. He wrote:

> Industrial missions still exist. But the Industrial Mission Movement in the United States is dead. Few mourn its passing. In fact its demise seems to have escaped the Church's notice altogether. Twelve years ago it was different. Our first industrial mission, based in Detroit, was celebrating its fifth birthday. At the trienniel convention of the Episcopal Church, held in Detroit that year, bishops and delegates alike crammed into buses and visited the

70

legendary production lines of Ford, G.M. and Chrysler. Bishop Wickham, whose industrial mission work in Shef- field, England laid out the basis for industrial missions around the world, addressed the Convention. And at the Convention the Episcopal Church, like other denomina- tions later, voted money for the furtherance of industrial missions.

End of liberal consensus

However, the reason for the failure of the initial strategy of the industrial mission movement is interesting and instruc- tive and herein may be its greatest potential contribution to the church. Though it was always difficult, working with industry and gaining a modicum of trust in the industrial milieu was possible in the days of the liberal consensus. Then almost everybody believed that through the industri- alising process continual progress was being made toward conquering the age-old curses of poverty, hunger, disease and toil. This promise would be realised not by human virtue but by the advance of technology, the improvement of management skills and the working of the economic system.

The huge accumulation of wealth and power that indus- trialisation had brought America and Western Europe was expected to become the general lot of mankind. This, we believed, could be achieved by concerning ourselves with the increase of wealth and not its distribution. With suf- ficient overall growth the condition of the poor would be inevitably improved. While controversy raged about the pace and methods of industrialisation and the distribution of its benefits, the acquisition of wealth and power became the universal goal of nations and the ambition, it seems, of most of mankind.

At its inception the industrial mission movement was part of this consensus. We criticised life in industry, it is true. We criticised it for its autocratic concentration of power at the top and for the stultifying routines and conditions of the production lines, for savageness in labour relations, management policies and union politics, for the inordinate commitment managers were required to make to their jobs. But we saw these as details. Basically we saw 'God's Hand' in industrialisation. We saw it as part of the process of humanising the world. And therefore we could affirm men's work in industry as fulfilling God's purpose.

By the end of the 1960s this consensus had broken down. Not only was the pace, the means and the distribution of the benefits of industrialisation in question but the goals themselves were in dispute. Industrial missioners, with one foot in the strongholds of industrial culture and the other in the Christian tradition, found their position increasingly ambiguous. My own rejection of the liberal consensus had its roots in my feeling that a discontinuity existed between a culture that dedicated itself to amassing wealth and promised affluence to all, and the religion whose founder declared that riches put a man in great danger and that the poor were blessed.

Ideological confrontation
On moving to Boston in 1965 to start a new industrial mission I found myself in an industry committed to developing ever more efficient and terrible means to kill people. So effective has this industry been that a handful of men now have the power to subject the earth and its people to an apocalypse without help of Divine intervention. My contact with scientists in the research and development industry also sensitised me to the destruction industrial culture was wreaking upon the earth itself. Although we in industrialised nations claim but a small fraction of the human race, our voracious appetite is so depleting non-renewable resources that neither the majority in poor nations nor future generations will have enough. And in our triumphant production and sybaritic consumption we are poisoning the world.

To raise these issues as being the fundamental questions facing civilisation today puts one outside the liberal consensus. And for an industrial missioner to press them insistently jeopardises his welcome in industry. He will be judged to be laughably irrelevant or subversive. For a great controversy has replaced consensus. The debate does not find some on the side of industrialisation and others wholeheartedly rejecting it. But rather some hold fast to the position that industrial culture is fundamentally sound, and others call for a profound change in the direction of industrial development. In the dispute about the primary goals for society the values of wealth and power are pitted against community and modesty.

It is certain that the leaders of industry and labour generally affirm the soundness of the present way. It may be inescapable that a relevant and authentic interpretation of the Christian tradition must opt for change. Trapped by this dilemma, industrial missioners either challenged the values of industrial culture and found themselves unwelcome adversaries in industry or endorsed it and began to lose touch with the Christian tradition.

British Industrial mission was, and is, a heroic, pioneering movement. Chaplains have gained entry into many of our principal industries. One of their great strengths is still the regular visiting of people while they are at work. Arising from this fundamental method of working has developed the study of a wide range of issues. Reports and initiatives have given new public insights into the thinking and activities of large companies. In this well-done and extremely honest work the conspiracy theory has begun to be challenged. There is the honest exploration of major practices and values in the light of the Christian faith. It is a cruel irony, but hopefully not a consequence, that many of the traditional heavy industries in which the chaplains were established have gone into decline.

The Don Valley in Sheffield, once the armourer of the Empire is now a shopping mall and sports centre. Chaplains have had to diversify and find homes in new industries. They also have had to fight for a home in a church where attitudes against 'specialists' have hardened. Chaplains suffer as church leaders and parochial clergy conspire against them. Companies in new industries with an international ethic and culture require missionary zeal on a new and sophisticated scale. A re-appraisal of their work was begun in 1988.[9]

Laity Centres

One form of conspiracy-blasting which has had a more lasting effect across Europe, though less so in England, is that of Laity Centres.

A stage between the worker-priest concept and that of the 'visiting chaplain' was practised in Germany by Horst Symanowski through the Protestant Gossner Mission. He took a job as a labourer in a large cement factory in Mainz Castel and for four years (1950–54) he devoted six months of each year to this work. During the summer months he gave his energies to building a centre to house what developed into a base for his industrial ministry. For this work he enlisted the help of many workers and several industrialists, as well as the help of over 500 young people from all over the world who took part in work-camps on the site.

The completed centre, called Gossner Haus could accomodate over 100 people, workers, industrialists, apprentices, seminarians, and many others who could explore together the implications of Christianity in an industrial society. The great contribution of this work to the field of industrial mission has been the establishment of these lay centres or 'academies' which now exist in other parts of the world. Here lay people can come together to take upon themselves the task of exploring the relationship of the Christian faith to modern industrial society.

These variations on conferences houses with their more 'hotel-like' equivalents in England have gone some way to creating a venue where people from many walks of life can discuss their work in an informed Christian atmosphere. In its own systematic way St George's House in Windsor Castle is a part of this work and has organised a series of conferences over several years with the general title 'Attitudes to industry'.[11]

The worker-priests, the industrial missioners and the pioneers of laity centres have made the most progress in exploring the conspiracy which has for so long separated corporate industrial and commercial activities from the Christian faith. Informed and socially aware lay people and clergy have worked away at this dialogue in a way that has influenced opinion-formers and those in the structures in industry and commerce. Codes of business ethics, a look at the responsible company, 'mission statements' and a range of reports and publications have been the result.

These movements are indeed the beginning of a success story, but one which has been blighted. There is always the persistent problem for all those concerned with contemporary ethics that events move so fast and technology develops so rapidly that the dialogues and solutions of one year appear outdated by the next.

The conspiracy in disguise

More significantly in the last twenty-five years two distractions have presented themselves. One is a misleading debate about secularisation; the other is the lobby inside and outside the churches for intermediate technology and the 'greening' of industrialised nations. The next two chapters will describe events in these two areas as they have unfolded and analyse the good and bad effects of the lobbying. There is much that is good and valuable in both distractions. We must allow them to be unpacked in order to discourage both sets of protagonists from becoming co-conspirators who are trying further to separate God from the real events of our everyday working lives.

Chapter Six

Is small beautiful?

Green issues and green politics have been at the centre of the shift of much public opinion during the 1980s. In our home communities we have moved from 'waste paper for the Scouts' to bottle banks and waste disposal sites which look more like parks than refuse tips. We save drink cans and not just their pull-tops. We insulate houses as a matter of course and no longer see double glazing as a convenient option to 'keep out the draughts' or to cut down external noise.

How has all this come about? What can be wrong with conservation? Does this heightened sense of ecological awareness enhance or contradict our conspiracy theory? The conspiracy is broken where churches, politicians and industrialists have succeeded in combining to create a new climate where lasting improvements to the quality of life have been made. The conspiracy works in an alarmingly subversive way where Christians are made to feel guilty about the jobs they do and where industrialists feel excluded from any possibility of dialogue and change. It is a comfortable, convenient, collusion for churches and conservationists to attack from afar, and for industrialists to want to be written-off as beyond redemption. Stereotyping is much easier when face-to-face meeting is studiously avoided.

Conservation and balance

To hijack a word from the conservationists, it is all a matter of balance. The appropriate size for our industries and the level at which they are allowed to affect the environment is a debate which has consumed another kind of human energy. We do still need some industries and public services to be organised on a large scale so that they can operate economically and provide a benefit to large populations. Supplies of gas or electricity have to be organised, or at least co-ordinated regionally and nationally. Hospitals, however owned, need to be of a certain size or within a group so that specialist care can be provided. Oil has to be refined and steel made on a scale which allows its production and distribution to be done so that the processes and prices are kept as economic as possible.

The awareness of the dangers of industrial pollution to the welfare of people in urban areas became topical in the 1960s. The way in which Clean Air Acts were able to remove smog and pollution from our cities was remarkable. The speed of the improvement was a very visible testimony to the changes that could be brought about by political lobbying. It proved a great success for a consortium of environmental groups. Similar things have yet to be done for our rivers.

Pressure for the improvement of the environment came from many groups with the churches coming alongside as partners. It was in the area of development, world development, that the churches were central. Major missionary societes had been keeping an awareness of the needs of 'underdeveloped' countries in the minds of church people for generations. Their greater interest in social questions linked with more sophisticated publicity from the 1970s onwards gave their case a high profile. Questions were raised about the way in which industries in 'poorer' countries should develop. Questions were also asked about the way it was felt that some of the major trans-national companies were making profits at the expense of the poor. From what we have explored already in this book we know also that there has always been a stream of Christian unease about the making of profit. The scale of profits made by some companies and the scandal of loans made to some developing countries fuelled both the medieval and the puritan Christian conscience.

This range of disquiet in certain sections of society across Europe and slightly later in the United States brought into the public arena real and important questions about the relation of rich and poor nations. There was genuine concern about the way in which rich nations were living at the expense of the poor, but it was very difficult, at least in the late 1970s and early 1980s to establish a real dialogue with industrialists about the problem. The conspiracy was entrenched and reinforced by many who were thought to be the very victims of industrialisation. In the late 1970s I organised frequent seminars in the Sheffield area and was met with a disarming response. Many company directors and sales managers told me that however sympathetic they were to the idea of selling labour-intensive, intermediate technology goods to developing countries, they were often told, only the very latest, high tech, high status, equipment would do even for countries genuinely poor. So, British, continental and American specialists and technicians found themselves in India, South America and Africa constructing semi-automated factories in areas of high unemployment with poverty all around. I was often told in those days that it was hard to be ambassadors for conservation and intermediate-technology, however persuaded my managers were by the arguments.

A change in the ecological climate

However the climate has changed through some major publications and pieces of lobbying — and as a result of some horrific industrial disasters like those at Bopahl and Chernobyl. The origins of our present guilt and the crisis of confidence about our Western style of life stem from the early 1970s when *The Ecologist* magazine published *A Blueprint for Survival*.[1] It preceded by a few months the publication by a group called The Club of Rome of *The*

78

Limits to Growth.[2] Both of these papers described with horrifying evidence the way in which the rapidly expanding consumer societies of the West were eating up reserves of energy and raw materials at a rate which would exhaust supplies within the lifetime of our children. These predictions were linked to statements about waste and pollution and to the fact that we were drawing many of our resources from developing countries to their disadvantage.

The answer proposed by this 'ecological' lobby was the establishment of a Stable Society. The argument was based upon the concept that a natural balance of stability could be established and that, if allowed to, one section of the created order would serve to balance the other.

The conditions thought necessary to bring about a stable society were set out in this way:

(1) Minimum disruption of the ecological processes.
(2) Maximum conservation of materials and energy — or an economy of stock rather than of flow.
(3) A population in which recruitment equals loss.
(4) A social system in which the individual can enjoy, rather than feel restricted by, the first three conditions.

The adoption of such a view involved the acceptance of a no-growth society which was in direct contrast to present development. The authors of this Blueprint accept that these proposals were radical and would take some time to implement. They went on to set out a seven point programme to bring in this stable society.[3]

These ecological arguments were followed in 1973 by a substantial criticism of Western industrial life by Dr E. F. Schumacher in *Small is Beautiful: a study of economics as if people mattered*.[4] The case argued there was similar to that in *The Limits to Growth* but it was applied by this economist and businessman as a direct criticism of industrialists who claim to have solved the problem of production.

A businessman would not consider a firm to have solved its problem of production and to have achieved viability if he saw that it was rapidly consuming capital. How then could we overlook this vital fact when it comes to that very big firm, the economy of Spaceship Earth and, in particular, the economies of its rich passengers?[5]

Schumacher's answer was 'The economics of permanence' which is similar in many ways to the ecologists's argument for a stable society. His method of achieving this situation was the acceptance of 'intermediate technology'. Such technology is a stage between primitive rural industry and advanced Western industry. It would solve the problems of starvation and gross inefficiency and also of large-scale inhuman factories. He hoped also that smaller companies would help restore full employment.

This ecological campaign was conducted with evangelical fervour. It won many converts principally among the middle-class, educated, affluent sections of society. The preface to *Blueprint for Survival* ended with this rallying call:

> Such a movement cannot hope to succeed unless it has previously formulated a new philosophy of life, whose goals can be achieved without destroying the environment, and a precise and comprehensive programme for bringing about the sort of society in which it can be implemented.

Talk of goals and of a philosophy of life presented a clear challenge to the churches. Many church leaders were already coming to share the criticism of industrial society voiced by their contemporaries in the academic and educational world. These church people often shared a common professional background; few church leaders have commercial backgrounds and even fewer come from industry. 1975 was the year when the churches gave public support to the ecological criticisms of society voiced by secular prophets in 1972.

Enough is enough

The Christian version of 'Small is Beautiful' was *Enough is Enough*[6] written by Dr John Taylor, former General Secretary of the Church Missionary Society, and afterwards Bishop of Winchester. Taylor seemed to be convinced by the Limits to Growth arguments to which he added his own understanding of the Third World's needs from his experience with CMS. What is most interesting is that he was able to construct a 'Theology of enough' to underpin the economic arguments.

It is worth setting out this theological construction because the ecological argument is non-Christian in origin. Taylor describes the Hebrew version of an ideal society and says it could be summed up in the word Shalom, 'something broader than "peace"; the harmony of a caring community at its every point by awareness of God. . . .Economically and socially this dream of Shalom found expression in what I call the theology of enough.' The Old Testament, he says, is full of condemnation of covetousness and greed (Jeremiah 22.13–17, Habbakuk 2.9–11), the New Testament similarly condemns ruthless greed, (Mark 17.21, Colossians 3.5). Conversely, the Old Testament talks of limited cropping, (Deuteronomy 22.9) and in the New Testament moderation is praised, (Phil. 4.4, Col. 1.16–17, 2 Peter 3.5–6). Taylor sees in this biblical vision the description of a stable, interdependent society.

In Church tradition, Taylor is also able to support his case. Relying on Tawney he shows how the Medieval Church attempted to counter exploitation. He quotes Aquinas on the law of contract: 'A contract is fair when both parties gain from it equally'. He reflects on the difference the implementation of this principle would have made on the lives of the Sri Lanka tea workers. He also describes how, with the rise of capitalism, many of the prohibitions on the taking of interest, and on exploitation in general, were abandoned.

For a Christian in Taylor's thesis the model of the Kingdom now would be an expansion of the concept of eucharistic living where all life would be seen as a thanks offering to God. The re-establishment of tithing would be a celebration of the Lord's generosity. Taylor's arguments gained wide acceptance in the churches, partly because of the respect he had already won through his perceptive articles in the CMS *Newsletter*, and partly because agencies like the missionary societies, Christian Aid, and Oxfam were moving church members towards this more radical view of their own society.

Our Christian future

Also in 1975 came a 'call' to the nation from the Archbishops of Canterbury and York. It asked, 'What sort of society do we want?' and 'What sort of people do we need to be in order to achieve it?'. These questions implied a criticism of society and of members in it. The questions did provoke considerable discussion within the churches and led to the eventual publication of a book of replies to the call, entitled *Dear Archbishop*.

More substantially, this call encouraged the British Council of Churches to establish their two year discussion programme, 'Britain Today and Tomorrow'. The programme had ten associated themes and culminated in a massive conference at Swanwick over the Spring Bank Holiday of 1978 and the publication of a summary of the tons of papers produced in a competent book by Trevor Beeson.[7]

Responses to the strong criticism of Western society have now begun to emerge. The ecological case has overtones of nature worship or even paganism about it. What should be the attitude of Christians to nature? Ours is a faith which goes from God to nature via man.[8] One of the accounts of creation in Genesis gives us stewardship of God's created order. 'God blessed them and said, "Be fruitful and increase in number; fill the earth and subdue it. Rule over the fish of the sea and the birds of the air and over every living creature that moves on the ground" '. Part of our human responsibility is to acknowledge that nature is to be ruled by us under God. This is the context in which God expects us to work out our vocation.

A spirited response

Since the publication of *The Limits to Growth* there has been valid criticism of the computerised model on which the study was based. The structure of the study was too simplistic and its results were misleading. Even that veteran campaigner in the cause of conservation, Bishop Hugh Montefiore, felt unable to add his signature to the eminent list of supporters placed at the front of the *Blueprint for Survival* because he could not agree with all its conclusions.[9]

Of *Enough is Enough*, the reviewer for the Industrial Christian Fellowship Quarterly said:

> We believe that God so loved the world that He is continually creating, redeeming and sustaining it. This means everyone and all things. It means individuals concerned with organisations and the relationships between them. It means all the structures of common life. It means international institutions, the national government, all industrial companies, trades unions and professional bodies. . . .And what does the individual Christian decide to do when he thinks about his role as citizen or manager or trades union official or a member of a professional body or a good neighbour? These are hard questions. Answers are not easy. But until the Church and Christians and Bishops think about them we shall be charged with being drop-outs, although John Taylor denies that we want to be.

Here is a fundamental question for Christians to answer. If we accept the Limits to Growth solution do we condemn ourselves to the fringe of society and to a position which condemns industrialisation? Or can we reshape our understanding of the vocation of Christians and the Church in society in such a way that we can bring this argument to bear in a more realistic way? It is to this question that we must return when we look more closely at Christian vocation in chapter eight.

The real division among Christians and between ecologists and other economic commentators has been over the question of growth. The case for zero-growth has already been explained. The case for continued growth, even within the constraints of an economic recession, inflation and an oil crisis has been put with conviction by far fewer Church people, and when they have attempted to do so have been branded as right wingers or as naive economists.

One recorded example of such a difference of opinion is that between David Edwards and Charles Elliott. Edwards, then a Canon of Westminster, was asked to prepare a booklet which he called *The State of the Nation*,[10] for debate by the Church of England General Synod in 1976. At the end of his survey he made out a case for economic growth in a final chapter called 'The right kind of growth'. 'Provided that it does not damage the environment, the workers or the community, economic growth is a good thing because it enables us to pay for what we want.' Edwards has since reinforced his case in a wide-ranging book called *A reason to hope*.[11]

Edwards' whole case was attacked in a most aggressive way by Dr Charles Elliott, then Senior Lecturer in Economics in the School of Development Studies in the University of East Anglia, in an article in the April–June 1976 edition of *Crucible*, the Journal of the Church of England Board for Social Responsibility. Elliott criticised Edwards' too simple economic analysis, his failure to recognise the conflicts inherent in our social system and his use of theology to support a case for responsible growth.

> If all theology can do is sprinkle holy water on our secular judgements, or give a brief nod in the Almighty's direction as a kind of coda, then it is not to be taken seriously.

Elliott wants a much more radical theology which will heighten people's awareness of the injustices of life. 'I happen to believe that theology is to be taken seriously because it is capable of transforming our perception of reality — past present and future'.

This discussion serves to highlight a division between church and people about economic and industrial life. In the same country with considerable intellectual force, it is possible to reach very different conclusions. For Christian lay people where is help in all this? Is the choice for them a similar one, either feeling guilty about working in such an exploitative society or being branded as a right winger? Must they adopt the values of the ecological counter culture, or can they be helped to see work in terms of a vocation which can be offered to God?

A more general response to the ecological lobby is now developing. If the world's population is to double by the year 2000, this is not a prediction of doom but an enormous challenge. There is the challenge to feed, clothe and house such a growth of population. Rightly mobilised we already have the resources to meet such a challenge. If increased standards of living for all are to be achieved there need not necessarily be a continued decline in Western economies. Increased standards of living mean new markets. Our problem is one of the economic and commercial redistribution of wealth. The Christian is called to speak words of truth about economic and social justice, not unconvincing words about growth or no growth.

The most important discussion about economic growth and international interdependence to reach the public in recent times has been the *Brandt Report*.[12] A group of internationally known figures were brought together by Herr Willy Brandt on ten occasions beginning in the summer of 1978 to compare the economic problems of the developed North and the developing South. The result was a set of recommendations which recognised how much one economy depends on another and which suggested a programme of international financial reform. Much of what was contained in the report had been said by pressure groups and church people long before. The fact that these proposals did not come from that quarter gave them all the more credibility. Christians have given general support to Brandt but have had little success in persuading governments to look at the proposals. In fact, the recession which began in 1974 has even made Britain and the USA cut their aid to developing countries.

Choices for Christian workers

For most Christians there is not the clear choice between remaining in the mainstream of industrial society or of opting out altogether and living an alternative lifestyle. They have to stay where they are. Consequently there is some obligation on the churches, having heightened this awareness in Christians, to support them through these tensions.

The debate continues with some fervour. Britain's economic decline and relatively high inflation in recent years has weakened the case for growth along traditional lines. The influences of Far-Eastern companies on styles of management has challenged the way employees are regarded within a company. The ecology lobby has had a considerable influence on mainstream politics with each of the principal British parties incorporating conservation into their manifestoes.

In one very intriguing sense the conspiracy between religion and industry has been overtaken by events. Where the medieval constraints of religion once controlled the practices of manufacturing and trade, moral constraints have taken their place. These stem from almost a 'spiritual' reverence for creation which had been lost in much of the Christianity of post-Reformation Europe.

The central question remains: how can Christians work with integrity in mainstream companies where there are conflicts of ethics, of business practice and now of under-standings of conservation. In an intriguing book, *Greening Business: managing for sustainable development*[13] published in 1991, John Davis, a former Director of Shell and a colleague of Schumacher, sets out in what may become a classic way for the 1990s a strategy for change. He outlines a programme which will allow high degrees of conservation accompanied by a programme of decentralisation. Davis argues with intelligence and experience. His ideas have been well received as offering a responsible way forward with the 'crankiness' of the enthusiasts ironed out.

We have moved far from chaplains mounting 'commando attacks' into industry. In societies where communication is immediate and where it is increasingly difficult for infor-mation to be concealed, companies are being forced to act in more responsible and accountable ways. But major questions continue to nag at the Christian conscience. There remain the great issues of justice between rich and poor nations and of how developing countries can best be helped.

There still seems no realistic way for developed countries to be able to continue their present luxurious, consumer-led, lifestyles *and* for forests and minerals to be conserved. Is there a way in which Christians can be encouraged to live responsibly and still take a full part in mainstream economic activity? There has to be. If not, a major force for change will be lost to world development. If not, Christianity will be impoverished as it is relegated even more to the sidelines of economic life. Christians need to be supported and encour-aged to play as full and responsible a part as they can in bringing about change within their companies.

Appropriateness not heresy

Small is not necessarily beautiful in itself but appropriate scales for production, marketing and for working conditions are vital. The alarmist predictions of the Club of Rome and of the Brandt Report did their work. They alerted many who otherwise would not have heard, to the impossibility of a conspiracy continuing which had kept public, moral and religious questions in a separate compartment from the 'morality' and values of trans-national companies for generations. John Davis says, 'As the age of the giant, entirely self-sufficient and excessively bureaucratic enterprise passes into history, a new world of work is being born'.[14] This new world will need a spirituality and a coherent ethic to sustain it. Christianity can make a central contribution. The final two 'liberation' chapters of this book will begin to point a way forward. A way which is based on the spirituality and actions of those who have laboured long in this moral crucible.

Chapter Seven

The springboard of secularisation

The other great modern conspiracy arises from the notion that secularisation will inevitably erode the place of religion in a developed society. There is no doubt that in poorer countries with a lack of mobility among the population, where education is not universal and where traditions are strong, religion plays a large and often central part in the life and structure of a people and that its place remains unchallenged.

In developed societies with easy communications, an education system with its own values, where people work away from their homes, farms, villages or towns, then there are significant challenges to the practice of a people's traditional religion. But does industrial development inevitably bring with it 'secularisation' glibly characterised by a decline in church attendance?

Great and often rapid social changes brought about by industrial and commercial development inevitably bring a threat to traditional ways of life. The cement which holds the social fabric of a village together can all too easily crumble when it has to bear the stresses of the complex structures of a city. The traditions and safeguards of family life cannot easily be passed on if grandma lives 200 miles away — or in Calcutta, Jamaica, or Marseilles.

Added to these local and family discontinuities are the new values and traditions which grow up within a company or an industry. These do not arise from the local community but are a necessary consequence of that trade or profession or of the manufacturing process itself. There is a strong sense of community among those in coal mining or steel making or the railways. Within a profession such as banking, accountancy or the law the practices and traditions which go with that way of life are part of the induction process for a newcomer, at one level as important as the professional and technical skills which will be learned.

A traditional and defensive religion will understandably find difficulty in holding its place within times of social upheaval or industrial development and change. All too easily the decline of religion has been blamed on the industrial changes which are taking place or on the new values which have arisen within a community. This process of the weakening or decline of religion has been given the name of secularisation, a convenient but often unfortunate umbrella word which has been made the scapegoat for a whole range of causes which have led to the decline of the practice of religion in developed countries.

Learning a new language

In every society people need to be able to tell stories to one another so that they can 'make sense' of the events which are taking place around them. There are no answers, at the level of our intellect or our emotions and feelings, which will explain in a completely adequate way why illness comes, why loved ones die, why friends betray, why jealousy destroys relationships, why children can be so different from their parents and so on. At the wider level of society questions of the nature and causes of floods, famines, earthquakes and disease have until recent times required non-scientific answers. On the world stage in this century we have had to accommodate our lives to the prospect or consequences of most appalling wars.

With the development of scientific knowledge and of mass communication the answers which religions have given to many of these imponderable questions have seemed inappropriate, or have been superseded by medical, scientific or social knowledge. Secularisation is the name given to the process by which sections of society and culture are removed from the domination of religions institutions and structures. Sociologists describe the ways in which a religion interprets life's questions to a society as 'plausibility structures'. When these break down, or are broken by social change, then a religion finds difficulty in communicating its central or 'sacred' beliefs to many outside the closed ranks of its adherents.

It is all too easy to conclude that because in industrialised areas churchgoing has declined, industry causes unbelief. This conclusion has been accepted all too readily by many in the churches who consider that the morality, cut and thrust, competitive, profit-oriented nature of industry is beyond acceptable levels of Christian behaviour. Many in industry have been all too happy to allow the churches to write them off. They have been able to develop working and trading practices without an external frame of reference. Dismissal by the Churches, if not leading to a quiet life, has at least removed one interfering group from what was seen as a closed process between management and unions (and on occasions the government). The unhappy result of this collusion about secularisation in the Christian west has resulted in a Church divorced from the main agents which are shaping and re-shaping society. It has led to industries which do not have a central belief in what they are doing and who have been overtaken by competitors with a strong code of ethics whose employees have a dedication to their industrial and commercial processes not known in Britain in modern times.

The challenge of secularisation

We now have to explore the relationship of industrialisation to religion in order to see if it is inevitable that religion will decline as society becomes more developed. It may be that an examination of which plausibility structures have broken down will help to reveal which answers are no longer adequate for modern societies, and which questions need to be addressed now if a religion is still to have any meaning to the majority of people in countries where industry and commerce produce a universal urban lifestyle.

We have already seen that in the Reformation debate about the lending of money at interest the reformed churches, while taking the question seriously, failed to develop an acceptable ethic for the use of money as a commodity in itself when used by bankers or industrial organisations. The system of ethics commended was based on the use, or lending, of money by individuals to individuals. There were not sufficiently developed stories, underpinned by a corporate Christian ethic, to convey Christian values for justice and responsibility in the new commercial culture. The corporate nature of a Catholic Church giving social coherence to a society was abandoned gradually to give place to the individual holiness of the pietistic denominations of the sixteenth and seventeenth centuries. We have seen the musing of John Wesley on a religion extolling virtues of individual hard work without the reasoning which would think through the responsible use of the wealth accumulated by that hard work.

We have seen how the Primitive Methodist minister Colin McKechnie was offering a pastoral ministry to individuals while his chapel stewards were facing dismissal and the loss of their homes as they fought for better conditions in the mining industry. There were individual victories where many union leaders were inspired and sustained by their local chapels. Equally there are accounts in almost every industrial town of churches and chapels being endowed by local industrialists. However, from whichever side achievement is seen, the lesson of history is that the war was lost. Tawney's study of the rise of modern capitalism and Wickham's survey of the churches in Sheffield both show that plausible interpretations of Christianity, with its consequent stories to convey Christian behaviour were not embedded in the new industrial communities. One of the principal conclusions of the religious census of 1851 was that more seats, free pews, needed to be provided in cities so that there was room for new populations to be able to sit down when they went to church! The point that was completely missed was that what was needed were real connections between the experiences of life in urban communities and the truths of the deeper meanings of life held locked in unopenable boxes by churchgoers.

Free Church or Anglican, they were developing a ritualism in services and an increasingly inclusive and esoteric language to speak of their faith. Non-churchgoers found it difficult to understand and impossible to interpret through a range of stories which would speak to their own experience, either of 'dark satanic mills' or of life in a 'green and pleasant land'. Religion developed a language of its own, a culture of its own, and was linked to old class structures and politics in Britain at a time when new wealth, social mobility and education were beginning to break these divisions down and tell new stories about the possibilities and achievements of economic progress.

A 'do it yourself' secularisation

Professor Peter Berger also maintains that religion in the West has 'secularised itself!'[1] As an unintentional result of the Reformation many of the symbols used in conveying religion were dismissed or abandoned. The consequence of this was that many agents, stories and images which until then had conveyed the concept of transcendence were swept away. Fortunately medieval church buildings, though 'cleared of their idols', have remained.

In the Reformed countries of northern Europe, though the rather elaborate shell of medieval religion remains, the empty plinths and limewashed walls show by very plainness the absence of the teaching aids which conveyed the path to the heart of religion for rich and poor alike. Belief became private. Aids to devotion, statues, ritual, wall paintings, like the high doctrine of the Church itself, were seen as obstacles which came between Creator and created.

The reaction to superstition and an unbalanced worship of the Saints and of the Virgin Mary achieved the end of purging the outward trappings of belief. For many reformers these moves were effective. The consequence of this cleansing of the Church was the disappearance of much of religious practice from everyday life. The Reformed Churches and later the Catholic Reformation unwittingly played an important part in the secularising process.

It may appear absurd, and in the modern multi-faith situation impossible, but imagine the change in atmosphere of a factory, office or laboratory if there were a Holy Water stoup at the door, a shrine to Our Lady in one corner and a genuine Patron Saint for each company, and that every other principal religion in the company had its equivalents!

Of course, this can never be the case and most of us would not want it to be so. But, if we are sure that all human endeavour should be offered to God, then we shall want to understand the place of a religion in a society which has in part become secularised and in other ways has secularised itself.

Equally it can be argued that religion has often played a formative part in the development and redefining of the life of a country or a community. I want to suggest four ways in which religion influences or prevents change in a community.

The formative role of religion in society

There have been many occasions in the development of commercial and industrial societies when religion has been formative. The over-arching conventions of the Middle Ages were put in place and held by the medieval church. The development and legitimation of nation states was made possible through the political freedoms which religion encouraged at various times in northern Europe in the fourteenth and fifteenth centuries. The freeing from a sense of guilt and the idea of the possibility of personal salvation was part of the liberation which was brought by the Reformation. The 'Protestant Work Ethic' which made a Christian virtue of hard work was essentially the product of a heightening of the conscience in relation to work. It was the 'new vocation' open to all, a calling to responsible living to be offered to God as the true path to salvation.

The legitimating role of religion in society

At this stage in our argument it would be absurd to suggest that any development in the life of a church can be separated from changes taking place in the society in which that church is set. Changes take place, like that of the widespread practice of usury and the Church adjusts to give a rather belated blessing, to give legitimation, to a practice already well established. Professor Robin Gill has instanced many cases of the churches recognising and blessing changes in moral practice rather late in the day, and without any apparent need to admit a change of heart.[2] Similarly, he suggests that subtle changes in attitudes to morals and to industry and to capitalism can be seen in various Papal Encyclicals over the past 150 years.

Religion as a dependent agent in society

Some religious changes in society do not arise from internal developments in education or economics but depend upon political events within a nation. Often they have had consequences for surrounding countries or countries who have received substantial immigrant populations. Professor David Martin in his book, *A General Theory of Secularisation*[3] describes how the place of a religion in a country can be dependent upon these political events in history. He describes how the outcome of the French revolution determined the place of religion in France. Similarly he sees the consequences of the American War of Independence as central in the relation of churches to the state in the United States. In the same way the outcome of the English Civil War has affected English religious life into this century. Religion was an important factor in these wars, their outcome has marked out the place which religion will have in each country. He maintains that the lives of churches are dependent upon certain events in history.

Religion as a defensive social agent

Most common of all is the role of religion as a conservative agent, defending a traditional way of life against the acids of modernity and change. Examples haunt the centuries. In this defensive function also the Church holds traditions, passed on through whatever 'plausibility structures' are available, moral teachings and the values of a faith. The holding of a tradition which is vibrant and alive and able to dialogue with change has much to offer in giving continuity and stability in times of rapid change. Churches which approach change with a living tradition to offer contribute much to a society. Churches which exist only to defend the traditions and practices of a previous generation for their own sake, will soon be left high and dry.

This cycle of the relationship of a Church to the society in which it lives can be described with this diagram.

The dynamics of secularisation

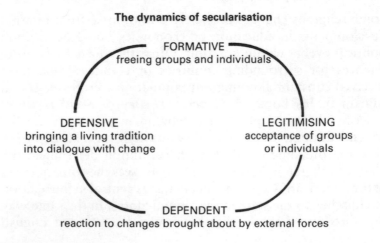

FORMATIVE
freeing groups and individuals

DEFENSIVE
bringing a living tradition
into dialogue with change

LEGITIMISING
acceptance of groups
or individuals

DEPENDENT
reaction to changes brought about by external forces

The springboard of secularisation

It is unfortunate that, in terms of religion, secularisation is always stated in negative terms. It is the modern heresy which undermines the practice of religion and consequently the possibilities for belief itself.

For us in the late twentieth century secularisation is the natural consequence of changes which take place in society. It is caused by the new values of industry and commerce; it is caused by the increased mobility of a population where roots and traditions can be left behind; it is caused by the pluralism which is the inevitable consequence of a mobile society; it is caused by the Churches themselves removing their symbols from the mainstream currents of society, and, no doubt, very much more. It is the combination of this range of changes which break down the plausibility structures of a society and prevent a defensive religion from making new inroads. Secularisation is a gift which those who do not want to dialogue with any religion will welcome with open arms. But this modern secularisation conspiracy must not be allowed to continue. The inevitability of its corroding effect on a religion has been exposed.

Secularisation neither invalidates the observance of religion nor the belief in God which religious practice and symbolism represent.

Two things are needed for the proper establishment of religion in a technological society:

— a spirituality which will convey religious images in a new and plausible way.
— a morality which will arise naturally from this spirituality and which can be sustained by it.

I shall explore these possibilities in the concluding two chapters. From the supposed terminal illness and death caused by secularisation can come resurrection through the re-discovery of a living God who comes to us through our traditions, our history and the stories we must tell to make sense of our life as we approach the beginning of the twenty-first century.

Chapter Eight

Spiritual Liberation

"THE time of business does not differ with me from the time of prayer; and in the noise and clutter of my kitchen I possess GOD in as great a tranquillity as if I were on my knees." So said Brother Lawrence as he went about his work in the monastery kitchen

The way to freedom from a conspiracy which is determined to keep work and Christian values apart is to develop a spirituality which sees life as an integrated whole. In a full understanding of God's creation there can be no parts which are separated off as areas in which Christianity has nothing important, or relevant, to say. No doubt most Christians would agree with this. Our task is to create a situation where divisions cannot creep in or, in places where they are long established, to create such an atmosphere that divisions seem contrived and artificial.

I propose to do this by strengthening our understanding of Christian spirituality in four areas:

— We need a spirituality of our activities where it becomes clear to us that everything we do, and especially our activity at work, can be offered to God.
— We need a spirituality of things. By this I mean we need to be able to offer the actual thing we do, or the thing we make, up to God. We offer not just our activity but what we are active in doing.
— We need a spirituality of places. Just as there are holy places for pilgrimage and holy atmospheres in churches or chapels, we need to set aside places in our holy buildings for thought and prayer about work.
— We need to rediscover a spirituality of our calling. We need to see that our calling is not necessarily to a particular job but a response, and a responsibility, to be Christians where we are, living our God's call of faith to us.

A spirituality of our activities

One of our team of industrial chaplains used to visit a well known Liquorice Allsort manufacturer based in Sheffield. In the course of a conversation with the transport manager the subject of integrating faith and work came up. The chaplain had been reading *The practice of the presence of God* where the seventeenth-century Brother Lawrence was explaining the idea that at all times, in whatever tasks, he would try to hold the idea that God's presence was with him. This so struck the manager that he went on to read the little book of conversations and letters by Brother Lawrence[1] and to publish a prayer and presence card which he distributed and made available to the chaplains. It is reproduced at the beginning of this chapter.

Here was someone who was seeking to break this conspiracy. He was concerned about the 'separate compartments' of his life and took up this idea of the practice of the presence of God to help integrate, to be the common thread, between home, leisure and work.

There is nothing new for Christians in wanting to see all of life integrated. We sing with great joy the wonderful hymn by George Herbert, 'Teach me my God and King in all things thee to see, and what I do in everything to do it as for thee'. Herbert with his poetic Anglican spirituality saw this harmony and wanted to celebrate God's presence in all things. But sentiment needed a school. Perhaps that is why he began with 'Teach me . . .' The result of the development of an integrated spirituality is shown in a later verse of the hymn, 'A man that looks on glass on it may stay his eye, or if he pleaseth through it pass and then the heaven espy'.

It cannot be easy to 'espy' the heaven in a serious and stressful piece of work, or in something dull and repetitive, or in a company taken over so many times that every sense of loyalty has been threatened, or in a company besieged by unhappy industrial relations. Industries, newly given that name, of health and education suffer from changes which leave many demoralised or feeling that the profession in which they began has changed, and changed them, often beyond recognition. Martin Wright's 'No' to industry with which I began may seem better for those who feel all spirit knocked out of them.

Such a negative response to industry and commerce demands firm action. There are many who will not be encouraged by the soft self-effacing prayerfulness of Brother Lawrence sufficiently to set out with realism on this new course of integration. I have seen the need for a response described well by someone who was not in the everyday heat of industry and commerce but whose life and writings, in spite of condemnation by his church, were concerned with seeing the wholeness of God's creation.

Père Teilhard de Chardin was an accomplished scientist and geologist, a Jesuit who worked and taught in France but principally in China. Towards the end of his life he set out to write a book of devotion about the interior life. It was published in 1957 with the title, *Le Milieu Divin*.[2] It had an intriguing dedication 'SIC DEUS DILEXIT MUNDUM — *For those who love the world*'. The first section of the book is called 'The divinisation of our activities' and makes an impassioned plea for dedication to this task of integration and not merely sentimental wishing. He says, 'I do not think I am exaggerating when I say that nine out of ten practising Christians feel that man's work is always at the level of a "spiritual encumbrance . . ." A few moments of the day can be salvaged for God, yes, but the best hours are absorbed, or at any rate, cheapened, by material cares'.[3] He went on to explore the seriousness of this discovery which was to him also the unmasking of a conspiracy which tried to keep the sacred and the secular in separate compartments. He was able to say, from his particular Roman Catholic background, that there were all kinds of groups dedicated to particular causes — charity, missions, liturgy, contemplation. Could there not be groups also dedicated through their lives to the task of 'Sanctifying human endeavour'. People who through their everyday activities could show the divine possibilities or demands which any worldy occupation implies. He wanted to see Christians who would devote themselves to occupations which his translator calls 'the very bonework of society'. They would show in their work some of the possibilities for worship and fulfilment normally reserved for more 'sanctified' occupations.

A spirituality redirected would look for the presence of God by deliberate prayerful discipline in all parts of working life. But to do this requires dedication and the deliberate offering up to God, with integrity and thanksgiving, activities and occupations our conspiracy theory has led us to believe hide the fullness of the glory of our Divine Creator. This would be a daring step on the road to the spiritual liberation of human work.

A spirituality of things

'He took bread' is a very appropriate way of saying that Jesus used the everyday, basic, things of life to demonstrate God's presence with us. 'He took Bread'[4] is the title of an essay by Kenneth Adams, Comino Fellow at St George's House, Windsor. In the opening section he makes an interesting observation when asking why Christians are so quick to attack materialism. He remarks that in the pages of almost any Christian newspaper there will be articles attacking the materialism of our age. Alongside them there will be advertisements for Christian Aid, Cafod, Tear Fund and others with accompanying pictures of starving children. There will be appeals for people to give of their material goods, in the shape of money or clothes, to help those who are so clearly in desperate material need.

This contrast puts sharply into focus the need to come to terms with materialism and a responsible use of the world's resources so that the technological knowledge we have can be used to raise the standard of living of all.

The Half-Cloak Project at St Martin-in-the-Fields is a controversial attempt to link the charity which made St Martin of Tours give half of his cloak to a beggar with the wealth and productivity which made the cloak. The project aims to develop a debate between those who create wealth and those who care for the poor.

'He took bread' brings us to the heart of our Christian spirituality in the Eucharist. Jesus brought together worldly, material, products of human work and by the way in which he used them, gave them profound spiritual significance. In this action he shows a unity of the material and the spiritual.

Jesus roundly condemned a solely materialistic approach to life. The parable of the farmer who, through good harvests, built larger and larger barns demonstrates this. He had hoped to accumulate enough wealth to be able to live the rest of his life in comfort. But the discovery of his impending death revealed the emptiness of placing confidence in the acquisition of riches.

Many others who have sought security in status, responsible jobs or large investments have discovered the same. These can all be swept away overnight, with one imprudent action, one wrong decision, or by a financial collapse.

Equally, a concentration on developing the spiritual life in isolation can have its dangers. In Jesus' parable of the Good Samaritan it is the Priest and the Levite, specialists in spiritual duties, who pass by the man who had been attacked. It is the Samaritan, quite possibly a businessman on a trading journey from Jerusalem to Jericho, who provides material care.

A spirituality of things gives us a heightened sense of responsibility for the use of material goods. It makes us aware of the importance and centrality of the right use of possessions in a balanced Christian life.

That is one aspect of a response. The other is in the things we produce. It is not adequate to say that we work in order to produce goods and create wealth so that the general standard of living in the world will be improved. Christians need to be able to offer up to God what they actually do or make.

Here, of course, there are serious moral problems about the nature of some products. Some work cannot be offered to God, though there is less of this than there may seem. Many ask questions of Christians working in the armaments industry; others say that the work of a prostitute or of a bookmaker are difficult for a Christian to defend. Within these extremes lie the very wide range of occupations which Christians do pursue. The conditions of employment, the culture of a company, the fierceness of the competition can also make life difficult, or exhilarating. They do not cut a person off from God.

'He took bread' gives a sacramental nature to the product

of human work. God's presence in the workplace, sought after and recognised by us, can give a similar sacramental understanding to all that we do.

I am pleased that in the communion services of all our denominations the offertory has a strong and visibly symbolic place. The bringing up to the minister of the bread, wine and money by members of the congregation links freely given goods with the offering of our talents. The prayer over the bread and the wine, 'Which earth has given and human hands have made', links nature, work and spirit in a most appropriate way. A spirituality of things ends our dependence on material goods. It is a window which opens to us a glimpse of the divine ways in which the fruit of our everyday activities can be used.

A spirituality of places

As a student on a solo trip to Rome, I can remember going down in St Peter's to the tomb of Pope John XXIII. I had visited many churches and shrines on my travels with my motor scooter and tent, but I was surprised when I came here. I went down the steps to the underground vault and experienced a stillness and a peace which was new to me. I was made aware that in all of God's creation there are special places which speak to people in particular ways.

In the previous chapter on secularisation I have referred in a dismissive way to the idea of having shrines for all faiths in factories and holy water stoups at the gates. I have been impressed by the idea of places being set aside for special prayer or intercession.

In the shell of the ruins of the old Coventry Cathedral 'hallowing places' have been created. It is said that a distinctive feature of medieval cathedrals was their guild chapels which were situated around the walls of the building. There smiths, girdlers, drapers, mercers, cappers and dyers would have their particular place of prayer. At Coventry this idea has been taken up in its modern form and has now been copied by other parish churches. In this way a spirituality for work can be given a home and a place where prayer and hopes and offerings can rest.

Such a spirituality of places is not confined to churches and shrines, indeed some of them have very little sense of holiness. Atmospheres are created by the people who use a place. I know well through years of factory visiting how very similar offices and departments can have quite different atmospheres according to the people who set the tone in a place. So, a spirituality of places is a powerful instrument to break the sacred and secular conspiracy. New dimensions can be discovered in the atmospheres created as people work together in particular places.

Here is the Coventry prayer for the hallowing places in their old Cathedral.

> Hallowing Places
> IN INDUSTRY
>   God be in my hands and in my making
> IN THE ARTS
>   God be in my senses and in my creating
> IN THE HOME
>   God be in my heart and in my loving
> IN COMMERCE
>   God be at my desk and in my trading
> IN HEALING
>   God be in my skill and in my touching
> IN GOVERNMENT
>   God be in my plans and in my deciding
> IN EDUCATION
>   God be in my mind and in my growing
> IN RECREATION
>   God be in my limbs and in my leisure

A Spirituality of our calling

At the heart of any spiritual reawakening about the place of work in a full understanding of our lives must be a strengthened understanding of vocation. It is a mistake to think of vocation only as a call to some special, and usually 'caring', piece of work. Vocation simply means God's call to each of us to live our lives as Christian people.

We must start, however, from the understanding of vocation which is known to most people. Teaching on this subject was the great contribution of Luther to the social ethic of his time. 'You can and must' he said, 'serve God in your daily calling as surely and as truly as in your religious acts.' In the face of monasticism this was a bold statement. The monk was no nearer God than the burgher or the farmer. The sanctity of daily duty was the great reformation principle for Christian living. Since that time the idea has been modified and even exploited until today the 'work ethic' has very little meaning and vocation has been relegated to the province of the caring professions. What can we say to the modern equivalent of the godly burgher or farmer?

In attempting to look again at vocation we must broaden the contemporary understanding of vocation to a profession, to a particular piece of work, or to the religious life. We are not looking at the secularised version of calling which the sociologist Max Weber described as a 'limited field of accomplishments'. Nor are we attempting to describe the justification and sanctification of all secular institutions, as some Lutheran theology has attempted to do in the past. There will always be some occupations that will not come within this description, just as some occupations were prohibited to members of the early Church. *A rule of thumb definition of the concept of vocation must be that the occupation contributes towards the building-up of God's Kingdom. In theological terms man's work must be able to be seen as contributing to God's scheme of Creation, making a full use of our God-given gifts and faculties.*

The best basis for a new beginning is to be found in what the New Testament has to say about calling. Paul, in his letter to the Corinthians says, 'Every man should remain in the condition in which he was called. . . . For the man who as a slave received the call to be a Christian is the Lord's freedman, and, equally, the free man who received the call is a slave in the service of Christ. . . . Thus each one is to remain before God in the condition in which he received his call' (1 Corinthians 7.20). Paul can say this because of his great understanding of the relationship of God to us which he describes in the letter to the Romans, 'A man is justified by faith quite apart from success in keeping the law' (Romans 3.28). So, a redefinition of the concept of vocation must be on these terms and not with the construction of a new law. No one is justified by faith in work, or faith in technology itself.

Dietrich Bonhoeffer in his *Ethics* says that vocation is to be understood primarily in the context of the call of Jesus to us, 'In the encounter with Jesus Christ man hears the call of God and in it the calling to life in the fellowship of Jesus Christ. Divine grace comes upon a man and lays hold upon him. . . . From the standpoint of Christ this life is now my calling; from my own standpoint it is my responsibility. . . . Now a man takes up his position against the world in the world; the calling is the place at which the call of Christ is answered, the place at which a man lives responsibly'.[5]

Here is food for a renewed understanding of vocation. It allows us to respond to God's call almost wherever we are. It is not an isolated personal response alone, because the 'calling' has to be worked out within the context of God's activity and within the responsibilities and constraints of real life. This is not an easy path to tread. Bonhoeffer says, 'The good and free conscience does not come from the fulfilment of earthly vocational duty as such, for here conscience continues to be wounded by the unresolved conflict between a plurality of duties'.[6] The path of Christian discipleship is rarely easy. In the frustrations of trying to work out the implications of Christian vocation, the imagery of the suffering of Jesus on the cross will often seem most appropriate.

In the dramatic circumstances of his imprisonment, Bonhoeffer was led to reflect, 'Christians range themselves with
God in his sufferings; that is what distinguishes them from
the heathen. As Jesus asked in Gethsemane, "Could you not
watch with me one hour?" That is the exact opposite of
what the religious man expects from God. Man is challenged
to participate in the sufferings of God at the hands of a
godless world. . . .It is not some religious act which makes a
Christian what he is, but participation in the sufferings of
God in the life of the world'.[7]

The challenge, then, is to lift work from being a 'spiritual
encumbrance', to being the place where we work out our call
from God to be a Christian. A renewed sense of vocation
does not see God in all things but sees all things as being able
to be offered to God. It sees radical criticisms of industrial
society as part of living responsibility. It sees also, in this
calling, the necessary responsibility to see the world as it is
and to continue to suffer with God in the transformation of
the world towards what it might become.

Chapter Nine

Ethical Liberation

There can be no such thing as ethical liberation. At least not in the sense of the burden of problem-solving and decision-making being lifted from us. As long as we live, have feelings, and can reason, we shall be faced with all kinds of questions and will have to make·a wide range of ethical decisions. There can indeed be liberation when we have a heightened awareness that we are making ethical decisions of the kind which will affect our future and the futures of those around us, and that there is a Christian framework which can support us. Ethical liberation in our working lives can come as we develop the ability to see the place of the Christian faith in our work and its importance in the decisions we make.

A sense of freedom can come to Christians when they are able to see, in the 'broad sweep' of teachings and behaviour in the Bible, principles and guidelines for their own actions. Biblical knowledge, a common familiarity with the stories and events of the Old and New Testaments cannot be assumed. Traditional methods of passing this knowledge on have largely disappeared. Believers have to work hard to gain an understanding of the events described by the biblical writers. An advantage of this is that the stories, and the revelations of God contained in them, come to many in a new and fresh way. Rarely, if ever, can teaching be lifted directly from the Bible and applied to a specific situation, but its pages do contain great moral principles which must be drawn out and used as a framework for everyday action.

A knowledge of the Bible, linked with a specifically developed spirituality is the basis for an ethical liberation from any conspiracy to keep work and religion apart from each other. A knowlege of the history of Christian thinking about work such as that described in this book comes as a necessary supplement. It gives a perspective to what often seem like totally new and unprecedented problems which hit us every day.

Liberation grows from our understanding that we are not compromised, or condemned, by our Churches and by many other Christians because of the kind of work we do. Liberation comes with our discovery that, within certain defined limits, Christians are free to live and work in any way which they feel gives them integrity and dignity. Liberation from a feeling of guilt imposed by the Churches or by other Christians can be liberation indeed. It is release from an internally imposed and restrictive bias. An ethical liberation which allows us to see our hitherto condemned occupations as ways in which we can offer a vocation to God opens wide the world of manufacturing and business ethics which the Churches had preferred to keep locked and bolted away.

If almost all we do can be offered to God, then the dimensions of achievement and spiritual fulfilment which this discovery offers are enormous indeed. To be able to offer up to God what we make, and how we make it, as well as the people we work with, is to make every day a harvest festival.

Everyday ethics and Reflective Practice

When describing in detail what I mean by ethical liberation I want to use a phrase, or a method, I have found helpful in working with lay people and with clergy when they review their working lives at about the half-way point. *Reflective Practice* is a way of deliberately standing back from the speed of everyday events and trying to gain a new perspective on what we are doing. The first step along the path of reflective practice is to try not to be carried along by the crowd when popular opinions are being expressed without first pausing to see if one really agrees with what is being said. Reflective practice allows a person to resist going along with the pressure of events, of 'the way we do things here', and to see if what he or she is being asked to do really fits with the way he or she is trying to develop as a Christian.

Trying to use reflective practice in being a Christian at work may take much patience, and will involve many frustrations and failures. The path will be different for each of us. It will wind on with slopes and hills and will have sharp bends and road repairs for all our working lives. However, it will not seem like a maze to be endured until release comes with retirement and perhaps time for 'more work for the Church'.

Many discussions with Christians in industry and commerce have led me to the understanding that there need to be certain 'core' elements in reflective practice for Christans. These include:

— An understanding of the nature of work itself from a Biblical standpoint.
— A Christian view of conflict.
— An affirmation of the centrality of wealth creation.
— An ease with the responsible use of profits.
— A strong critique of the consequences of industrial production for the relief of the world's poor.
— The necessity to develop codes of practice for industrial and commercial enterprises.

A biblical understanding of the nature of work

Work is both a penalty and a privilege. As with many other profound questions about life, answers or models are found in the first chapters of the Bible. Chapters 1–11 of Genesis contain stories which are sometimes called 'myths'. In a literal form they address questions which each generation asks about why things are as they are.

Very early on in Genesis, in the two interwoven stories of the Creation, work is seen as a privilege. Two people God created are seen as stewards of Creation, both masters and participants in the continuing work of Creation. This is described in chapter 1.26–28.

'God said "Let us make man in our image, in the likeness of ourselves, and let them be masters of the fish of the sea, the birds of heaven, the cattle, all the wild beasts and all the reptiles that crawl upon the earth". God created man in the image of himself, in the image of God he created him, male and female he created them. God blessed them saying to them, "Be fruitful, multiply, fill the earth and conquer it. Be masters of the fish of the sea, the birds of heaven and all living animals on the earth".'

A little further on, work is seen as a punishment and is explained as a consequence of disobedience to God in what is called 'the Fall'. Genesis chapter 3.17–19 describes this:

'Accursed be the soil because of you. With suffering shall you get your food from it every day of your life. It shall yield you brambles and thistles, and you shall eat wild plants. With sweat on your brow shall you eat your bread, until you return to the soil, as you were taken from it. For dust you are and to dust you shall return.'

So, what we know to be true from our experience of work is placed in a divine setting by these creation stories. Work can be exciting and fulfilling. We can genuinely feel a creative sense of pride in much that we do. But work can also be painful, we feel that however hard we try it yields only brambles and thistles. Work can be tedious and repetitive. Some of this drudgery is of our own making; some is inevitably tedious because anything worth having or making will require a lot of hard work.

Our basic attitude to labouring, both its creative and

frustrating sides, is set out for us right at the beginning of the Bible and gives us a helpful perspective as we look at what is actually contained in this mixed blessing which we call the world of work.

A Christian view of conflict

It is quite understandable that many people should want to shy away from conflict; it is part of our human make-up to do so. Our minds try to forget painful experiences as soon as possible. When a strike is over people want to forget about it and get back to work. This is all good and natural but it is of no help when the next strike or time of conflict comes around. It is the bitter and destructive side of conflict which Christians, along with all others, find difficult.

There is conflict in plenty in the Bible and there are a number of ways in which it is faced and resolved. André Dumas in his study *Political Theology and the Life of the Church*[1] gives us a whole series of accounts of conflict within human relationships. He chooses to look at brotherhood as a particularly Hebrew concept.

Cain murdered Abel (Genesis, chapter 4) and received a curse from the Lord — like the Devil in the book of Job, he was condemned to be a wanderer on the face of the earth. But with the curse went also 'the mark' which would protect Cain from being murdered. In the very long term we come to understand that this allowed Cain's descendents to be reconciled with those of Seth, Abel's substitute. In this protracted reconciliation God protects the guilty party and has patience with the destroyer. The harm he has done is so great that it can only be put right by future generations. For Cain, no forgiveness is offered or received but the possibility of a future reunion is maintained.

In the case of Jacob and Esau (Genesis, chapters 27–33) it is Jacob who tries to bring about a reconciliation. Jacob has robbed, deceived and humiliated Esau. Years after, Jacob wrestles with the angels of God (Genesis 32.38) and then attempts a reconciliation with his brother. This is done in three stages. He uses diplomacy, by sending presents. Then, surprisingly, at the reunion it is Esau who falls on his brother's neck to embrace him. However, when Esau suggests that they continue on their journey together, Jacob is wise enough to know that in the long term the memory of old grievances may overshadow the emotional effect of the reunion.

This second example goes somewhat further than the first since a reconciliation has been achieved. However, the reconciliation is such a fragile one that each brother decides to settle a long way from the other. Here the 'spirit' of the resolution of conflict is kept but in practice little is achieved.

The third example is one where conflict is resolved in a way which brings about complete reconciliation. It is that between Joseph and his brothers (Genesis, chapters 37–45). Joseph, the wronged party, offers reconciliation in a spirit which is able to forget all past grievances. Here Joseph has the chance to take revenge on his brothers who long ago had sold him as a slave but instead Joseph sees in this unexpected reunion a Divine opportunity for reconciliaton. 'I am your brother Joseph whom you sold into Egypt, do not be distressed because you sold me here: for God has sent me before you to preserve life' (Genesis 45.5). Jacob interprets events as the working out of Divine Providence. In this third example not only is complete reconciliation offered and received, but also the possibility for new growth is restored. The new relationship between the twelve brothers establishes the basis for the development of the confederacy of the twelve tribes of Israel.

However interesting these examples from the Old Testament are, for most people the attitude of Jesus to conflict will be the best known and the more often discussed. Jesus spoke about conflict in his parables. There is plenty of conflict in the parable of the labourers in the vineyard and in that of the Prodigal Son. However, we have in the life and death of Jesus a most vivid account of how he anticipated, faced, and resolved conflict. The story of Jesus' ministry is one of increasing conflict between himself and the various religious and political bodies who were confronted by his message. His life is an acted parable about conflict. His reaction to conflict is interesting — he must press on with his ministry, with the proclamation of his message, yet he is well aware of the consequences of his actions. There would be more conflict which could well end in his death. Parallel to this, when people were confronted by Jesus they were shown up for what they were. Some could accept this and consequently their lives were changed. Others could not; they harboured resentment and eventually brought about Jesus' death. God's handling of these events vindicated Jesus' action and released the powerful energy of resurrection which has been a force discovered by Christians ever since.

Conflict is hard to handle, especially when you are in the same office or workshop with difficult people every day. The bearing and offering of this up to God begins to ease the tension. These biblical examples show that sometimes we can resolve a conflict by our own actions and new relationships can be established. Sometimes a conflict has to be endured for a very long time, as well as faced, before any resolution can come.

Other conflicts occur when changes are being brought in to a work situation that seem thoughtless and unreasonable at the time. Facing these changes with whatever discussion and representation is allowed requires courage, endurance and an even temper! We cannot always see what is right for us, or for a company. Sometimes changes can only be brought in by dramatic intervention from outside. Conflict and death may have to come before any kind of resurrection.

One of the most difficult situations of conflict arises when there is a moral or ethical disagreement about the way a company or a department is being run. Rachel Jenkins for the William Temple Foundation has written a study about the conflict which she experienced as leader of an Adult Education department in a local authority when financial cuts forced her, the only full-time staff member, to lay-off many part-timers who relied on their income to support their families.

She writes of a search for a morally acceptable and practical solution, and a search with others for a spirituality which would support those caught up in that public sector conflict. She speaks of 'alliances' formed to give strength to those in similar situations, and instances times when reasoned responses brought about policy changes. She speaks also of how some in these 'alliances' learned to accept the unalterable and to acknowledge, and to mourn, the pain of loss.[2]

A Christian affirmation of the centrality of wealth creation

There has always been in our Christian religion a bias towards austerity, self-denial and a life of simplicity and poverty. Yet without others working to provide food and clothing, buildings and material goods, we would not have many of the life-giving, life-sustaining, qualities of our modern society.

So, Christians do have to ask themselves whether the wealth-creating work of industry and commerce is in itself a right ethical activity for them. Is the 'creation of wealth' as good an activity as direct involvement with healing the sick?

What is wealth creation? By our work, some say, in five basic activities — hunting, farming, fishing, manufacturing and mining — we produce all that we need for human existence. Through the means available to us in our modern industrial activity we are able to produce a surplus from any of these five basic activities. In the process of making things, or of hunting, farming, or fishing we can accumulate more than we need, or by industry make things for other people to use.

The process of wealth creation is the production of surpluses linked with the selling of goods and distributing them. Trading is the buying and selling of the goods and the investment in the manufacturing process itself.[3]

These trading processes are open to abuse. The availability of huge sums of money offers the possibility of large fortunes being gathered and of much corruption. There is ample evidence throughout history of the abuse of wealth and the power it brings.

This abuse is in part linked with the separation of wealth creation from any codes of moral behaviour. The greater the wealth the greater the possibilities of corruption.

But the need to create wealth in order to establish or sustain a reasonable standard of living for others has to be an activity which Christians can affirm. It is held to be equal with the direct healing of the sick if the creation of wealth is understood as a responsible service to the rest of society. Making the surgical instruments, providing buildings, homes, electricity and all the rest is a service. Christianity would have an unjust bias if it regarded those in these wealth-creating activities as fulfilling a vocation any less than those in the caring or teaching professions.

An ease with the responsible use of profits

Much public Christian discussion displays an unease with the idea of making profits on goods produced. Nothing can be made and sold only at cost, as those in developing countries know only too well. 'Added value' has to be given to a product to reflect its real costs. These have to include fair wages for employees, returns for further investment, returns for those who invest in a company, the cost of reasonable advertising and very much more. Book publishers need this added value, book sellers need to exceed their costs and even authors need to be paid! The concept of profit goes with an affirmation of the processes of manufacturing. Christians, alongside all others, have to make enough profit for their businesses to continue and to expand.

As with the abuses of wealth-creation, it is the *excessive* making of profit which has to be criticised and brought within some acceptable range of ethical standards.

A strong critique of the consequences of industrial production for the lives of the world's poor

The tremendous contribution which the Missionary Societies, the World Development Movement and many other groups and agencies have made to our understanding of industrial production is an understanding that it can have serious adverse consequences. We have been made aware that the use of raw materials by developed countries at much less than a fair price has kept many Third World countries in a continued state of under-development. A critique which defends the rights of the poor and the under-privileged has rightly been developed by Christians in this century.

Equally we have been made well aware, through the Intermediate Technology movement that many of our methods of production are wasteful of human and material resources. We have been encouraged to realise that in creating new industries and in establishing new industries in developing countries many of the mistakes which we have made need not be repeated. Christians involved in industry and commerce have been made starkly aware of these problems through publicity and from much preaching.

A heightened awareness of the abuses of production has to be set alongside the great benefits which have resulted. Christians need to be supported by their churches as they bring an awareness of this Christian critique of industry and commerce to the places where they work. Escaping to so-called more morally defensible jobs is often a hollow victory

— no more than exchanging one set of moral dilemmas for another. Ethical liberation for those in industry and commerce comes with a heightened understanding of some of the problems of their work and its consequences and the knowledge that other Christians are prepared to stand alongside them and support them through the moral dilemmas which any really satisfying job will provide.

The necessity to develop codes of practice for industrial enterprise

Where can Christians turn for immediate help and support as they try to put their faith into practice in their working lives? One of the most encouraging features of business ethics in recent years is that Christians of all denominations have combined to develop analyses of industrial and commercial organisations. They have often been able to work with companies to help them devise their own codes of practice. The work of the industrial missioners has been very influential in companies across Britain. Institutes such as the William Temple College in Rugby and, after its move, in Manchester continue to act as a focus. Scottish Churches House at Dunblane between Edinburgh and Glasgow, the Luton Industrial College and St George's House at Windsor are also pioneers in this work. Christian Fellowships within companies, though tending to emphasise a more personal faith, can also support Christians in their work. The Industrial Christian Fellowship is a national organisation with a long history of providing support for lay people in their jobs. It produces a Quarterly Journal and regular papers for its members.

Sometimes these organisations do need a little searching out but most are listed in the *U.K. Christian Handbook* which is available in all large libraries.[4]

For my own part I have put together a list of qualities which I would want to see in any job:

— At least a minimum of variety.
— The option to go on learning.
— At least a small area of decision-making.
— A degree of colleague support on the job.
— Recognition of the job's contribution to the purpose of the company.
— Some prospect of development or promotion.
— A just wage or income.

Conclusion

Ethical liberation does not give definitive answers for Christians to tell them what they should do in any particular situation. Times and issues change very rapidly making answers given to last year's problems look very old-fashioned indeed.

Ethical liberation as developed in the whole of this book can show us:

— That we have been victims of conspiracies to keep work and the Christian faith apart. Their exposure can bring liberation from guilt and captivity and an informed freedom to think and act in new ways.
— Escape comes through perspectives. Christians, in the world but not of it, have another frame of reference.
— Reflective practice brings the Christian tradition into dynamic interplay with a range of current questions about working life.
— The conspiracies are exposed. The challenge now is for us to be able to live responsible Christian lives where our work can be offered to God in an equal way with all else.

Ultimately, for Christians as for everyone, what we do, make or earn should help to enrich our spiritual lives. Liberation from Unholy Conspiracies comes with the discovery that, with God's help, the Christian faith can bring new freedoms for each of us, even in our working lives!

Notes

Chapter One

1. *English Culture and the Decline of the Industrial Spirit 1850–1980*, Martin J. Weiner, Cambridge University Press, 1981.
2. See, *The Clerical Profession*, Anthony Russell, SPCK, 1980.
3. Weiner, p. 116.

Chapter Two

1. *Religion and the rise of capitalism*, R. H. Tawney, Pelican, 1972.
2. *The protestant ethic and the spirit of capitalism*, Max Weber, Translator T. Parsons, Allen & Unwin, 1930.
3. *The life of the Revd Colin McKechnie*, J. Atkinson, Mitchell, 1898.
4. *Church and people in an industrial city*, E. R. Wickham, Lutterworth, 1957.
5. op. cit., p. 264–5.

Chapter Three

1. Terry Coleman, *The Railway Navvies*, Pelican, 1968, p. 22.
2. Dick Sullivan, *Navvyman*, Coracle, 1983, p. 5.
3. op. cit., p. 206.
4. op. cit., pp. 210–11.
5. See A. R. Vidler, *The Church in an Age of Revolution*, Pelican, 1961.
6. See F. Maurice, *Life of F. D. Maurice*, 1884, Vol I, Macmillan, p. 458.
7. E. R. Norman, *Church and Society in England 1770–1970*, Oxford, 1976, p. 171.
8. C. F. G. Masterman, *Life of F. D. Maurice*, Vol II, Murray, 1907, p. 35.
9. A radio talk given in 1949 and later published in *Ideas and beliefs of the Victorians*, Sylvan Press, 1950, p. 118.
10. Ed. Charles Gore, *Lux Mundi*, Murray, 1890, pp. 300–1.
11. For a view that Green's influence was less than was originally thought see, A. M. Ramsey, *From Gore to Temple*, Longman, 1960 and Peter Hinchliff, *Jowett and Gore; Two Balliol Essayists*, Gore Lecture, 1983. Reproduced in *Theology*, Vol LXXXVII, July 1984, No 718.
12. G. L. Prestige, *The Life of Charles Gore*, Heinemann, 1935, p. 228.
13. Footnote 5 in *Gore, a study in Liberal Catholic thought*, James Carpenter, Faith Press, 1960, pp. 244–5.
14. Prestige, p. 280.

15. op. cit., p. 408.
16. M. B. Reckitt, *Maurice to Temple*, Faber & Faber, 1946, p. 163.

Chapter Four

1. *Christianity and social order*, William Temple, Penguin, 1942. Republished 1976 by SPCK with a foreword by Edward Heath.
2. *The army and religion*, YMCA, 1920.
3. *Rhymes*, G. A. Studdert Kennedy, Hodder & Stoughton, 1922.
4. *William Temple*, W. A. Iremonger, Oxford, 1948, facing p. 544.
5. *Not ceasing from exploring*, Peter Sedgwick, C of E Board for Social Responsibility, 1987.
6. *Dog Collar democracy*, Gerald Studdert Kennedy, Macmillan, 1982.
7. See *The Malvern Conference Declaration*. Republished in 1991 by the Industrial Christian Fellowship, with a foreword by David Arthur.

Chapter Five

1. *France Pagan?*, Abbé Godin, Translator Masie Ward. Catholic Book Club, 1949
2. *The Church and Industrial Society*, Gregor Siefer, DLT, 1964.
3. op. cit., pp. 81–2.
4. *Industrial Mission in Sheffield revisited*, Philip Bloy, Sheffield Industrial Mission, 1987.
5. *The Task of the Church in Relation to Industry*, Church Information Office, 1959.
6. *Church and People in an Industrial City*, E. R. Wickham, Lutterworth, 1957.
7. *Church and People thirty years on: a historical critique*, Jeremy Morris, Theology, Vol XCIV, March/April 1991, No 758, p. 92.
8. *Requiem for American Industrial Missions*, Scott Paradise, Audenshaw Papers No 41, 1974.
9. *Industrial Mission: an appraisal*, C of E Board for Social Responsibility, 1988.
10. *The Christian Witness in an Industrial Society*, Horst Symanowski, Translator G. Kehun, Collins, 1966.
11. *Attitudes to Industry in Britain*, Kenneth Adams, St George's House, Windsor Castle, 1979.

Chapter Six

1. Vol 2, No 1, 1972. Revised edition published as a Penguin special, 1972.
2. MIT Press, 1972.
3. *A Blueprint for Survival*, p. 30.
4. *Small is Beautiful*, E. F. Schumacher, Abacus, 1973.
5. op. cit., p. 11.
6. *Enough is Enough*, John V. Taylor, SCM, 1975.
7. *Britain Today and Tomorrow*, Collins, Fount, 1978.
8. *Religion and the Persistence of Capitalism*, R. H. Preston, SCM, 1979, p. 50.
9. *Taking our Past into our Future*, H. Montefiore, Collins, Fount, p. 226.
10. *The State of the Nation*, D. Edwards, CIO, 1976.
11. *A Reason to Hope*, D. Edwards, Collins, 1978.
12. *North-South: a programme for survival*, Pan, 1980.

Notes

13. *Greening Business: managing for sustainable development*, John Davis, Blackwell, 1991.
14. op. cit., p. 107.

Chapter Seven

1. *The Social Reality of Religion*, Peter Berger, Penguin, 1973, p. 117.
2. *Beyond Decline: a challenge to the churches*, Robin Gill, SCM, 1988, pp. 22f.
3. *A General Theory of Secularisation*, David Martin, Blackwell, 1978, pp. 4–5.

Chapter Eight

1. *The Practice of the Presence of God*, Brother Lawrence, Epworth, 1959.
2. *Le Milieu Divin*, Teilhard de Chardin, Collins, 1960.
3. op. cit., p. 65.
4. 'He took bread', Kenneth Adams. Privately circulated, 1984.
5. *Ethics*, Dietrich Bonhoeffer, Fontana, 1964, p. 255.
6. op. cit., p. 257.
7. *Letters and Papers from Prison*, D. Bonhoeffer, Fontana, 1959, p. 122.

Chapter Nine

1. *Political Theology and the life of the Church*, André Dumas, SCM, 1978, chapter 2.
2. *Changing Times — Unchanging Values?*, Rachel Jenkins, William Temple Foundation. Occasional Paper No 20, 1991.
3. I am grateful to Mr Kenneth Adams, Comino Fellow for Industry at the Royal Society of Arts for the substance of this argument.
4. *U.K. Christian Handbook*, MARC Europe. Published every two years.

Bibliography

Adair, J. *The becoming Church*, SPCK, 1977
Atkinson, J. *The life of Revd Colin McKechnie*, Mitchell, 1898
Baelz, P. *Ethics and belief*, Sheldon, 1977
Berger, P. *The social reality of religion*, Pelican, 1967.
Pyramids of sacrifice, Pelican, 1977
A rumour of angels, Pelican, 1971
The heretical imperative, Collins, 1980
Bonhoeffer, D. *The cost of discipleship*, SCM, 1959
Ethics, Fontana, 1964
Letters and papers from prison, (enlarged edition) SCM, 1971
Catherwood, H. F. R. *The Christian in industrial society*, IVP, 1964
A better way, IVP, 1975
de Chardin, T. *Le Milieu Divin*, Fount, 1964
Dumas, A. *Political theology and the life of the church*, SCM, 1978
Edwards, D. *Religion and change*, Hodder, 1969
Leaders of the Church of England 1828–1944, Oxford, 1971
A reason to hope, Collins, 1978
Galbraith, J. K. *The affluent society*, Pelican, 1958
Gill, R. *The social context of theology*, Mowbray, 1975
Prophecy and praxis, Marshall, Morgan & Scott, 1981
Beyond decline, SCM, 1988
Habgood, J. *Church and nation in a secular age*, DLT, 1983
Hewitt, G. (ed) *Strategist for the spirit, Leslie Hunter, Bishop of Sheffield 1939–1962*, Beckett, 1985
Higham, F. *Frederick Denison Maurice*, SCM, 1947
Hodson, H. V. *The diseconomics of growth*, Pan, 1972
Howe, E. M. *Saints in politics*, Allen & Unwin, 1971
Iremonger, F. A. *William Temple*, Oxford, 1948
Jackson, M. J. *The sociology of religion*, Batsford, 1974
Macleod, G. F. *Only one way left*, Iona Community, 1956
Martin, D. *A sociology of English religion*, Heinemann, 1967
A general theory of secularisation, Blackwell, 1978
Martin, R. B. *The dust of combat: A life of Charles Kingsley*, Faber, 1959
Munby, D. L. *The idea of a secular society*, Oxford, 1963

Norman, E. R. *Christianity and the world order*, Oxford, 1979

Norak, M. *The Spirit of Democratic Capitalism*, I.E.A. and Madison Books, 1991

The Victorian Christian Socialists, Cambridge, 1987

Preston, R. H. *Religion and the persistence of capitalism*, SCM, 1979

Reckitt, M. *From Maurice to Temple*, Faber, 1946

Richardson, Alan *The Church of England and the First World War*, SPCK, 1978

Roberts, C. A. *These Christian Commando Raids*, Epworth, 1945

Russell, A. *The clerical profession*, SPCK, 1980

Scott, C. *Dick Sheppard*, Hodder & Stoughton, 1977

Schumacher, E. F. *Small is beautiful*, Abacus, 1974

Siefer, G. *The Church and industrial society*, DLT, 1964

Tawney, R. H. *Religion and the rise of capitalism*, Pelican, 1972

Taylor, J. V. *Enough is enough*, SCM, 1975

Temple, W. *Christianity and world order*, Penguin, 1942. Republished with a foreword by Edward Heath, SPCK, 1976

Van Buren, P. *The secular meaning of the gospel*, SCM, 1963

Velten, G. *Mission in industrial France*, SCM, 1968

Wiener, M. *English culture and the decline of the industrial spirit, 1850–1980*, Pelican, 1985

Wickham, E. R. *Church and people in an industrial city*, Lutterworth, 1957

Encounter with modern society, Lutterworth, 1964

Index